D1600311

LIBERIA AND SIERRA LEONE

An Essay in Comparative Politics

BOOKS IN THIS SERIES

1 *City Politics: A Study of Léopoldville, 1962–63* – J.S. LA FONTAINE
2 *Studies in Rural Capitalism in West Africa* – POLLY HILL
3 *Land Policy in Buganda* – HENRY W. WEST
4 *The Nigerian Military: A Sociological Analysis of Authority and Revolt, 1960–67* – ROBIN LUCKHAM
5 *The Ghanaian Factory Worker: Industrial Man in Africa* – MARGARET PEIL
6 *Labour in the South African Gold Mines* – FRANCIS WILSON
7 *The Price of Liberty: Personality and Politics in Colonial Nigeria* – KENNETH W.J. POST and GEORGE D. JENKINS
8 *Subsistence to Commercial Farming in Present Day Buganda: An Economic and Anthropological Survey* – AUDREY I. RICHARDS, FORD STURROCK and JEAN M. FORTT (eds.)
9 *Dependence and Opportunity: Political Change in Ahafo* – JOHN DUNN and A.F. ROBERTSON
10 *African Railwaymen: Solidarity and Opposition in an East African Labour Force* – R.D. GRILLO
11 *Islam and Tribal Art in West Africa* – RENÉ A. BRAVMANN
12 *Modern and Traditional Elites in the Politics of Lagos* – P.D. COLE
13 *Asante in the Nineteenth Century: The Structure and Evolution of a Political Order* – IVOR WILKS
14 *Culture, Tradition and Society in the West African Novel* – EMMANUEL OBIECHINA
15 *Saints and Scholars: Essays in the Organisation of a Senegalese Peasant Society* – DONAL CRUISE O'BRIEN
16 *The Lions of Dagbon: Political Change in Northern Ghana* – MARTIN STANILAND
17 *Politics of Decolonization: Kenya Europeans and the Land Issue, 1960–1965* – GARY B. WASSERMAN
18 *Muslim Brotherhoods in Nineteenth Century Africa* – B.S. MARTIN
19 *Warfare in the Sokoto Caliphate: Historical and Sociological Perspectives* – JOESPH P. SMALDONE
20 *Liberia and Sierra Leone: An Essay in Comparative Politics* – CHRISTOPHER CLAPHAM

LIBERIA AND SIERRA LEONE

AN ESSAY IN COMPARATIVE POLITICS

CHRISTOPHER CLAPHAM

Senior Lecturer in Politics
University of Lancaster

CAMBRIDGE UNIVERSITY PRESS

CAMBRIDGE
LONDON · NEW YORK · MELBOURNE

Published by the Syndics of the Cambridge University Press
The Pitt Building, Trumpington Street, Cambridge CB2 1RP
Bentley House, 200 Euston Road, London NW1 2DB
32 East 57th Street, New York, NY 10022, USA
296 Beaconsfield Parade, Middle Park, Melbourne 3206, Australia

First published 1976

Printed in Great Britain
at the University Printing House, Cambridge
(Euan Phillips, University Printer)

Library of Congress Cataloguing in Publication Data

Clapham, Christopher S.

Liberia and Sierra Leone

(African studies series ; 20)

Includes bibliographical references and index.

1. Liberia – Politics and government. 2. Sierra Leone – Politics and government.
3. Political sociology. I. Title. II. Series.
JQ3929.A15C58 301.5'92'09664 75-32447
ISBN 0 521 21095 X

To the memory of Anthony Clapham
1910–1973

CONTENTS

MAPS, TABLES AND FIGURES

Maps

Tables

Figures

PREFACE

This study has been in my mind since I paid a first visit to Sierra Leone and Liberia in 1969, and was struck by the possibilities which they offered for political comparison. I should like to thank the Department of Government at Manchester for making that visit possible, the Department of Politics at Lancaster for giving me leave of absence for a longer visit in 1973, and the Social Science Research Council, London, for meeting travelling expenses for both. I have benefited greatly from discussions with colleagues and friends at both Manchester and Lancaster, at Fourah Bay College in Freetown, at the University of Liberia in Monrovia, and at Cuttington College, Gbarnga, Liberia; seminar discussions at Oxford, London, Edinburgh, and the University of the West Indies, Jamaica, have also been most helpful. Dennis Austin, Bill Tordoff, Caroline Tutton, and CUP's anonymous reader made very useful comments on the draft.

I greatly appreciate the amount of help which I received from many Liberians and Sierra Leoneans: Ministers, Representatives, Paramount Chiefs, government officials, village schoolmasters, journalists and many more. I can remember none who were not friendly and courteous, and few who did not go out of their way to provide me with information and enlightenment. I should also like to record my debt to that neglected band of scholars, the writers of unpublished theses, and in particular to Walter Barrows for his work on Kenema, Victor Minikin for that on Kono, and Martin Lowenkopf for that on Liberian central politics; these and other obligations are more fully recorded in the notes. Finally, I wish to thank Lyn Hunter for typing successive drafts of the manuscript.

Lancaster
June 1975

C.S.C.

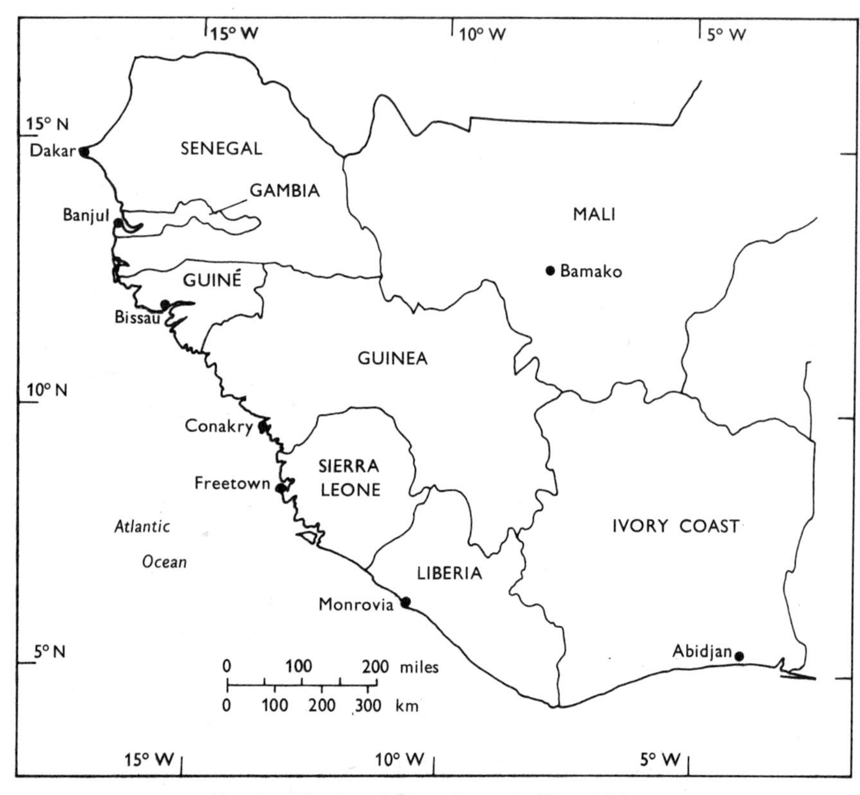

Map A. Liberia and Sierra Leone in West Africa.

CHAPTER 1

POLITICAL COMPARISON

Political comparison is an activity more preached than practised. Despite the centrality of comparison to the study of politics, despite the number of comparative frameworks which various authors have produced, and despite the amount of material on individual political systems which is now available, the number of studies which compare in any detail the ways in which politics works in two or more polities remains astonishingly small.[1] Yet if political comparison is to improve our understanding of the particular, rather than merely piling up generalisations, this is precisely the kind of task which it should be able to undertake. This is what the present study tries to do, in comparing the politics of two neighbouring West African states, Liberia and Sierra Leone. I hope to be able to show how (and, in a limited way, to explain why) some aspects of politics are very similar in the two countries, whereas others are notably different. More especially, I am concerned with the relationship in each country between political activities directed towards controlling the coercive and distributive apparatus of the state, and the social and economic features of the society on which that state is built. This relationship in turn has implications for many critical issues in the politics of underdeveloped countries – the colonial legacy, control of the economy, regime stability and institutionalisation, the role of elites – though in an essay such as this, such implications can only be sketched in a highly tentative manner.

There is a lot to be said for comparing entities which are fairly similar to one another. It is perfectly possible to compare an elephant and a bedbug, and any discoverable similarities between the two will tell you a certain amount about the properties common to living organisms. They are unlikely, though, to tell you anything very interesting about elephants or bedbugs which you did not already know from looking at these creatures on their own. Much the same consequences are likely to follow from comparing, say, the politics of the USSR with those of a Bergdama band.[2] But Liberia and Sierra Leone have already so much in common that it is plausible to suppose that the experiences of each may help to illuminate the other. They share the peculiar legacy of Creoledom, and the late nineteenth-century expansion from the coastal settlements into a hinterland itself divided between numerous ethnic groups; they have analogous administrative hierarchies, and distributions of educational and professional skills; and they have similar economies, based principally on the export of primary materials – especially minerals – by foreign-managed corporations, and only relying to a secondary extent on indigenously-produced cash crops. The sharp break comes in the political legacy of colonialism in Sierra Leone and of long independence in Liberia. There are no controlled experiments in politics, least of all at the level of national comparisons. But at least the similarities and differences may be marked enough to give some impression of the impact of direct colonial rule, and more broadly of the extent to which alternative political heritages may order differently the common elements in the social environment of two underdeveloped West African states.

But even if two countries appear to be inherently comparable, the simple juxtaposition of relevant facts from the experience of each is not enough to do the trick. It is also necessary to construct a framework which places these facts in some ordered relationship, and thus makes it possible to compare political processes between polities, without wrenching them from the context which gives them meaning. This is the problem which any political comparison faces, and numerous approaches have been devised in attempts to solve it: Eastonian systems analysis, structural-functionalism, game theory, and various forms of Marxism, are among the more familiar. The solution adopted here stems from the idea of politics as regulated conflict.[3] Politics, in this approach, is seen as being primarily concerned with the ways in which conflicts arise in society, the ways in which they are organised, and the ways in which – however temporarily or unjustly – they are resolved. These elements are brought together through the activities of politicians, who seek – whether by promoting conflicts or by trying to resolve them – to maintain their own positions and gain access to the prizes which the polity has to offer: power, and through it, the allocation of wealth, status, and yet more power.

To achieve these goals, politicians must involve themselves in a number of closely related activities. First, they must identify those *resources* in their environment, access to which may be useful to them. Political influence, after all, does not float freely, like a bubble waiting to be grasped by the most agile politician; it is gained by politicians who succeed in associating themselves with appropriate elements in the surrounding society. These elements may include popular support, and the mobilisation of those identities, such as class or ethnicity, through which this is achieved; they may include special skills or status, such as those gained in many African states by membership of a chiefly lineage or access to western education; they may include control over organisations, such as the armed forces; and they will certainly include economic influence, in the form of control over productive capacities, or more simply the possession of cash.

But it is not enough for any would-be politician merely to identify and attach himself to a collection of resources. He must also discover how to use them. The point here is that resources are not automatically incorporated into political life, in such a way that so much money or so many votes equal so much political influence. They are incorporated through *rules*. Rules determine what the prizes are in the system, and how they may be competed for. They include both formal constitutional provisions, and informal values and conventions which equally affect the allocation of political power. They thus establish the marketplace and the terms of trade through which resources may be converted into political prizes.

A close relationship therefore exists between resources and rules, and a dividing line between the two concepts ultimately becomes hard to draw. Two points about the relationship need to be borne in mind. Firstly, resources logically require some set of rules for converting them into prizes. Secondly, simply by establishing the 'terms of trade', rules invariably and inevitably favour the holders of some resources at the expense of the holders of others; thus, there is likely to be conflict between actors seeking to change the rules so as to favour the resources which they themselves hold – in Hobbes' terms, 'to use for trump on every occasion, that suite whereof they have most in their hand'.[4] This conflict may take the form, either of attempts by those who control the formal apparatus of government to change the formal rules so as to disfavour opposition, or else of attempts by those who control hither undervalued resources to overturn some at least of the existing rules so as to give these resources a higher weighting. This is most obviously the case with a military coup, in which the soldiers displace the rules which maintain a civilian government in favour of alternative rules which give prominence to control by the army; in doing so, they will need to rely on the existence of informal rules which make this substitution acceptable, at least to a group of people sufficiently large or influential to enable them to retain their prize. In a more muted way, much argument over electoral systems derives from attempts by politicians to maximise the prizes which the disposition of their electoral support can give them.

The picture of political life which emerges from this approach is that of a mass of overlapping competitions, to which some structure and continuity is given by the organisation and persistence both of rules and of those interests which can be mobilised as political resources. It gains its attractiveness as a vehicle for comparison from the opportunities which it gives for combining comparisons at three levels of political explanation.

Firstly, the concept of resources provides a framework for comparing those elements external to the polity which feed through into politics. Though in any particular arena some resources may derive directly from political organisation – the control of an administrative or party apparatus, for example – ultimately resources derive from outside: from the social cleavages which define communal identities, from values which define the nature and limits of political participation and authority, from economies which define interests and create the organisations to express them, or from external political systems which influence the domestic arena. In different societies and economies, then, different resources are potentially available for political mobilisation, and the first concern of political comparison must be to compare these: to compare, say, the relative roles of ethnicity in two societies, or the effects of industrialisation in creating in one society interests which do not exist in another. The use of political resources as an organising concept helps to emphasise, moreover, that these societal variables are of interest to the political scientist only because, or in so far as, they may be used as bases for political activity.

Secondly, the concept of rules provides a framework through which to compare more specifically political variables: the role of institutional arrangements and the constitutional distribution of power in allocating prizes between the controllers of different resources. One would look to rules to explain why political systems with apparently similar resources may nonetheless behave differently in terms of their stability or the kinds of actors who win the major prizes. The importance of rules in allocating prizes is open to dispute. One school of thought tends to assume that the holders of certain resources – most often economic ones – will automatically acquire political power which they can use to shape rules to their own convenience; others, such as those who view political development in terms of institutionalisation, regard rules as at least potentially independent variables which may play an important part in structuring the process of political competition.[5] The distinction between rules and resources does not prejudge the issue, but provides a means through which it can be examined.

Thirdly, the competition of political actors for prizes combines both rules and resources in terms of a model of purposeful political activity. It thus provides a motive element which is missing from many comparative political schemes, and makes it possible to compare the ways in which actors behave under differing circumstances. There is an implicit assumption of rationality here: that politicians' behaviour is determined by their attempts to acquire the resources which they need to gain the prizes which they are seeking. This is a questionable assumption; politicians generally seek multiple and to some extent conflicting prizes, they act within the context of differing perceptions, and they possess differing political skills in trying to realise their goals. However, they must seek (and sometimes win) prizes if they are to stay in business at all, and their efforts to do this impose a certain discipline on their activities.

This is not the place to defend or to evaluate this approach. Its usefulness will be tested by the extent to which it illuminates the politics of Liberia and Sierra Leone, and the proper place to examine it is at the end. There is one basic point, however, which it is only fair to make clear at the start. I do not believe that it is possible either to measure resources or fully to codify rules. Nor do I believe that it is possible to elaborate and test any general concept of political rationality. The explanations which these concepts can give are therefore essentially limited. To those who require their explanations to follow deductively from tested hypotheses stemming from general theoretical laws, this book will thus not 'explain' politics in Liberia and Sierra Leone at all, but will merely seek to describe it. This does not bother me. Comparative politics has in my view been dogged by vain attempts to measure the unmeasurable and to establish testable general law explanations which are not simply practically difficult, but logically unsound.[6] I see no reason why the discipline should be tied to the pursuit of a scientific chimera. If political comparison provides some understanding of how and why the common activities of politics differ from or resemble one another in different political systems and situations, then in my view it has served its purpose.

The next chapter briefly outlines the history of both countries, to provide a factual framework to which later discussion can be related. Chapters 3 and 4 establish the general structure of comparison, dealing first with resources and then with rules, and showing how these relate to one another. The following three chapters follow the resulting themes into three areas of political life, comparing firstly the operation of the central governments, then politics at the local level and its relations with the centre, and lastly the distribution of economic resources and the ways in which these are incorporated into political life. Finally, the Conclusion sums up the main differences and similarities between Liberia and Sierra Leone, discusses the kinds of stress to which each is most vulnerable and those which each is best able to overcome, and provides an opportunity for assessing the theoretical approach.

CHAPTER 2

HISTORICAL SUMMARY

THE ORIGINS OF STATE FORMATION

The two neighbouring republics of Sierra Leone and Liberia are among the smaller West African states. Squeezed in between the Atlantic Ocean and the formerly French territories of Guinea and the Ivory Coast, they cover no more than 43,000 square miles for Liberia and 28,000 for Sierra Leone, with respective populations of some 1½ and 3 millions.[1] They are hot, wet, and for the most part low-lying. The whole of Liberia and the southern half of Sierra Leone lie within the West African forest belt, ensuring a plentiful rainfall, and many rivers drain down from the Guinea highlands across both countries to the swampy coast.

This rather inhospitable coast was the scene of a peculiar experiment in colonisation. The modern states of Liberia and Sierra Leone both owe their origins to the position of 'free persons of colour' in the United States, Great Britain and the British possessions in America during the late eighteenth and early nineteenth centuries.[2] In each case one solution to what was seen as the problem of free blacks in a white society was repatriation to Africa. Colonisation societies were set up, and the first settlements were founded on headlands which provided an anchorage safe from the West African surf. Freetown in Sierra Leone was established in 1787, and Monrovia in Liberia in 1822. Subsidiary settlements were set up at Sherbro in Sierra Leone and at intervals down the Liberian coast from Cape Mount to Cape Palmas. The original settlers were supplemented in Sierra Leone by slaves captured at sea and liberated by the British and other navies, and in Liberia by further immigrants from the United States and the Caribbean. The numbers tailed off with the ending of the slave trade and American emancipation in the third quarter of the nineteenth century.

The descendants of these essentially similar communities were known as Creoles in Sierra Leone and as Americo-Liberians in Liberia – terms which are still useful though they need to be used with care due to the mingling of the settlers with indigenous African peoples. They shared a common attachment to Western standards in religion, education and dress, and for the most part sought positions at first in trade, and later increasingly in the professions: teaching, the Church, the law, government service, and politics. The consciousness of these standards, and at times the need to defend their settlements militarily against the indigenous peoples, helped to create a sense of Creole or Americo-Liberian identity which persists, and finds expression within each community in institutions such as churches and masonic lodges.[3]

The main difference between the two settlements was that Sierra Leone was founded under British supervision whereas Liberia was under American, and this difference was to be crucial. Britain retained an interest in the settlement, especially as a naval base for operations against the slave trade, and the peninsula on which Freetown stands became a Crown Colony under a British Governor. The United States had few interests on the African coast, its attitude towards Liberia had all the ambivalence derived from the Negro problem in American politics before the Civil War, and it refused to regard Liberia as anything more than a private venture under American supervision. The settlers were therefore obliged to declare themselves an independent sovereign state, especially in order to protect their ability to regulate foreign commerce, and this they did in 1847.

As a result, the Americo-Liberians were able to develop a political system which, though formally derived from the United States constitution, was in practice closely based on the values and structures of their own community. They were not subordinated, externally, to any colonial power, nor did they need to take much account, internally, of the political structures of the indigenous peoples. In Sierra Leone, on the other hand, the Creoles never acquired full control over their own government, and were much less well placed than their Liberian equivalents to manage and profit from the expansion into the hinterland which took place in both territories at the end of the nineteenth century. By the time the colonial government ultimately withdrew, it had introduced further rules into the system which decisively affected the political position of the Creole community.

EXPANSION INTO THE HINTERLAND

The coast on which the settlers landed was not uninhabited. Successive waves of migration from the savanna lands in the interior had driven peoples further into the forest until ultimately they reached the sea. The classification of these peoples is hazardous, fragmented as they were into numerous small groups and polities, with few defined boundaries between them: the terms by which they are known owe as much to the classifications and political arrangements of the subsequent national governments as they do to the peoples themselves.[4] The most fragmented were those who filtered into the high forest of what is now south-eastern Liberia, and are known as Grebo, Krahn, Kru and Bassa; these speak related languages, and were governed through small chiefdoms or segmentary lineage systems; between them, they comprise some 37% of the modern population of Liberia. Most of the rest of Liberia, and the southern half of Sierra Leone, are inhabited by peoples whose languages fall into the Mende group, and whose political arrangements are characterised by small chiefdoms based on ruling families, and by the secret societies known as Poro. In Liberia, these comprise nearly half of the population, including the Kpelle – the largest single ethnic group in the country with 20% of the total – and other peoples such as the Mano, Loma, Gbandi and Vai. In Sierra Leone, they include the Mende, with some 31% of the country's population, and associated smaller groups. The chiefdom structures have been much affected by internal warfare and national government, but the Poro remains, a combination of cultural society and political association whose importance is still little understood. The northern savanna area of Sierra Leone is occupied by peoples possessing closer links with Guinea and Islam; the dominant group here are the Temne, with some 30% of Sierra Leone's population, and others include the Limba with about 8½%, and smaller groups such as the Loko, Koranko and Susu. Other peoples such as the Kono, in eastern Sierra Leone, do not fit into any of the main categories.[5]

From this brief and simplified summary, two salient facts emerge. Firstly, no single ethnic group dominates the hinterland of either country, though the Temne and Mende each comprise over half the population respectively of the north and south of Sierra Leone. Secondly, there has been no indigenous chiefdom structure capable of resisting the incursions or the administrative arrangements of the coastal power; there is no equivalent whatever to the Ashanti Confederacy, the Yoruba kingdoms, or the Sokoto emirates.

This fragmentation eased the task of the settlers and colonial government as they made their way inland. The Sierra Leone Colony had a long history of involvement in the affairs of native peoples up and down the coast and the expansionist ambitions of the more active Governors had been held in check only by Colonial Office caution. The Liberians for their part had long claimed a 'Manifest Destiny' to control and civilise the peoples of the interior. Not until the last years of the nineteenth century was there any attempt at effective occupation, and by this time both settlements were hemmed in by French expansion in Guinea and the Ivory Coast. The Freetown hinterland was annexed in 1896, under the title of the Sierra Leone Protectorate; this immediately provoked resistance, in the Hut Tax War of 1898, but by the early years of the twentieth century the area was pacified and an administrative structure set up. In Liberia, the same process was more protracted; central control was steadily extended under Presidents Arthur Barclay (1907–12) and Daniel Howard (1912–20), and completed in the early 1920s, often against considerable opposition.[6]

This expansion into the hinterland greatly increased the countries' populations and their natural resources, and involved the creation, sooner or later, of new structures to deal with both of these. The indigenous African peoples who now became part of the enlarged political unit greatly outnumbered the settlers, who by the early 1960s comprised less than 2% of the population of each country.[7] In each country, the hinterland peoples were subordinated to an alien government from the coast; but in Liberia, this meant a government of Americo-Liberians, whereas in Sierra Leone it meant, overwhelmingly, one of British colonial administrators. The Sierra Leone Protectorate was administered separately from the Freetown colony, through a Protectorate Administration based on Bo, and the familiar colonial hierarchy stretching down from the Governor through Provincial and District Commissioners to the Paramount Chief. After numerous changes between 1896 and 1946, this eventually comprised three Provinces, twelve Districts, and nearly a hundred and fifty Paramount Chiefdoms; the colonial administrative divisions have been maintained unaltered by the Sierra Leone Government since independence.[8] The Liberians made a similar distinction between the administrative arrangements for the old settlements and for the hinterland. The former were divided into five Counties, which sent Senators and Representatives to the Monrovia legislature and enjoyed an appreciable amount of local autonomy. The latter was ruled directly by Commissioners appointed from Monrovia, eventually comprising – again after many changes – three Provinces, ten Districts, and over a hundred Chiefdoms.[9] Certain areas on the coast, inhabited by Bassa, Kru, and Grebo peoples, were separately administered as Territories. In 1963–4 the hinterland was reorganised into four Counties, as part of a series of changes aimed at putting the indigenous peoples formally on a par with the coastal settlements.

ECONOMIC AND SOCIAL CHANGE

The main economic role of the coastal settlements even before the annexation had been as centres for trade with the hinterland. This trade was greatly extended after the incorporation of the hinterland into the administrative structures based on Freetown and Monrovia, since it then became possible to systematise the growing of cash crops, and to provide a framework for the exploitation of mineral resources. Both countries have 'underdeveloped' economies. They export primary produce to Europe, North America and Japan, and import mainly manufactured goods in return; trading networks are well developed, but the local manufacturing sector is small and weak. The economies have developed, rather, through the extension of the cash sector and through changes in the primary products exported and the economic structures needed to produce and process them.

Early trade was based on simple peasant crops such as kola nuts and palm kernels, which produced the bulk of Sierra Leone's exports into the 1930s. Between the wars, these started to be displaced by products which required complex corporations which were largely owned and managed from abroad. In Liberia, the Firestone Plantations Company, under an agreement made in 1926, established large rubber plantations to meet the demand for car tyres; other plantations followed, and rubber remained by far the most important Liberian export until the mid-1950s. It still accounted for 12½% of Liberian exports by value in 1972, but has long been overtaken by iron ore, which was rapidly developed from the 1950s onwards as a result of the 'Open Door Policy' for encouraging foreign investment. This is now mined by several consortia with American, German and

Swedish capital and management, and nominal Liberian participation, and in 1972 comprised 78% of Liberian exports.[10] Iron ore mining in Sierra Leone started in the 1930s, with the Sierra Leone Development Company (Delco), a subsidiary of William Baird of Glasgow, but with 13.7% of exports in 1971 it has never attained the same importance as in Liberia. The dominant position in Sierra Leone is taken by diamonds, with 60% of exports by value in 1971.[11] The equivalent corporation, Sierra Leone Selection Trust (SLST), is a subsidiary of the international Consolidated African Selection Trust (CAST) group, and has had to compete with armies of private (and generally illicit) competitors in the often anarchic conditions of the Kono and Kenema diamond fields. In 1971 the Sierra Leone Government took a 51% stake in SLST, which then changed its name to Diminco. Other exports include coffee and cocoa in both countries, and timber in Liberia.

Though the structures of the two economies are similar, Liberia is appreciably the richer. During the 1950s, Liberia had one of the fastest rates of economic growth in the world, averaging about 15% per annum for leading indices between 1954 and 1960.[12] Much of this was due to investment in iron ore mining, and the rate slackened to about 6½% per annum in the 1960s, about the same as the rate for Sierra Leone.[13] This left Liberia with a Gross Domestic Product of US $417m in 1970, against Sierra Leone's $451m.[14] When allowance is made for Liberia's smaller population, the per capita GDP is double that in Sierra Leone, at $357 against $177 in 1970.[15] This difference is only very partially due to government policy, though to some extent Liberian land tenure and produce marketing arrangements, and the welcome given to foreign investment, may have encouraged greater productivity than in Sierra Leone. Since a large part of the national income in both countries is derived from mineral extraction, it is little more than fortuitous that in Liberia the resulting wealth has to be divided among fewer than half as many people. One important way in which this difference feeds through into politics is in the government's revenues, and its consequent ability to provide economic pay-offs; in 1970, the Liberian government's consumption expenditure amounted to $45.3m, or $39 per capita, while the equivalent figures for Sierra Leone were $37.4m and $14.7.[16]

These economic developments have involved hinterlanders in the cash economy, and have been accompanied by the spread of communications and education, and movements of people into mining and plantation areas and the coastal cities. Road transport has expanded rapidly to link most population centres in both countries, though several settlements on the Liberian coast remain inaccessible except by air and sea. Education has increased to the point where, on the governments' latest available figures, 175,572 pupils were at school in Liberia in 1973, and 201,372 in Sierra Leone in 1970–1, some 13% and 8% respectively of the total population.[17] Employment opportunities have drawn people in Sierra Leone especially towards the diamond areas and Freetown, and in Liberia to the rubber plantations, the iron ore mines, and Monrovia, resulting in some areas in a decline in agriculture. The impact of education and urbanisation has however been by no means as great as in southern Nigeria or Ghana, and social change in the hinterland has generally been contained within the structure of the chiefdom at the rural level, and a small number of urban centres. Initially, too, a high proportion of educated hinterlanders, especially in Sierra Leone, were related to chiefly ruling families and so helped to maintain continuity within what has been called the 'traditio-modern elite'. In Liberia, the absorption of educated hinterlanders into the governing elite has similarly – and again perhaps only temporarily – helped to mute the politically disruptive effects of social change. The main exception has been in the diamond areas of Sierra Leone, where illicit mining since the 1950s has created a large, shifting and often lawless immigrant population.

The same economic changes created opportunities for new foreign immigrant groups, mostly in the trading sector. The banks, the major import-export businesses, and the mining and manufacturing enterprises are mostly run from Europe or America, though the political position of the Americo-Liberians in Liberia gave them also some opportunity for participation. Lebanese and Syrians who reached Sierra Leone in the 1890s and Liberia in the 1920s, have squeezed out their local competitors and established a monopoly over retail trade and produce marketing which governments are now trying to prise open; in Sierra Leone they also acquired a powerful role in diamond dealing. Guineans have arrived in large numbers to take over jobs in petty-trading, tailoring, taxi-driving and so forth. Political changes and economic demands in both countries since the early 1960s have raised the question of the political and economic status of all these alien groups.

POLITICAL DEVELOPMENTS SINCE 1945: LIBERIA

Liberia in the last thirty years has been governed by only two Presidents. William V.S. Tubman was inaugurated in January 1944, and after serving his initial eight-year term and being re-elected for five subsequent four-year ones, died in office in 1971. The Vice-President, William R. Tolbert, then succeeded to the Presidency. These two names, and the unbroken tenure of power of the only effective political party, the True Whig Party, since 1877, sufficiently indicate the personal and institutional stability of Liberian government up to the present. This continues to be based on the networks of faction and family among the coastal elite.

Within this framework of continuity appreciable changes have taken place, resulting from an appreciation by the coastal elite, and particularly by Tubman, that continued stability depended both on economic development and on broadening the political base of the regime. These two objectives were closely linked. Tubman's call in 1948 to 'strike the rock of our natural resources so that abundant revenues may gush forth'[18] put the first of them with a characteristically Liberian blend of cupidity and biblical phraseology, and the expansion in political participation since 1944 has largely been made possible by the revenues produced by the Open Door Policy.

The key to increased participation was the Unification Policy, which ostensibly aimed to break down all barriers between the descendants of the settlers and the indigenous peoples, and in practice offered to selected hinterlanders the opportunity of taking part in politics on terms approaching – though not entirely equalling – those available to the immigrant core. In pursuing this policy, Tubman held Executive Councils for the redress of grievances throughout the hinterland, thus presenting the President, for the first time, as President of all Liberia rather than simply of the coastal communities. In 1963–4, formal equality was achieved by abolishing the provincial system of hinterland administration, and creating in its place four new Counties with administrative structures similar to those of the five long-established Counties on the coast; this change was more than symbolic, since it allowed the new Counties representation in the legislature (where however they were still outnumbered by the representatives of the coastal ones) and greatly increased the number of jobs available for hinterlanders in their home areas.

Opportunities for increased participation did not extent to political activity outside the True Whig Party and the system of centrally administered patronage over which Tubman presided. Even when formally within the bounds of constitutional politics, this has been equated with treason, and suppressed. In 1951 a Kru, Didwo Twe, challenged Tubman's bid for re-election, but was obliged to flee the country before the poll. In 1955 Tubman was challenged by a splinter party, the Independent True Whig Party, led by his predecessor as President, but this also was outlawed; some of the party's supporters attempted to assassinate Tubman shortly afterwards.[19] More recent oppositional movements have been derived either from plots within the armed forces or from attempts to mobilise opinion in the hinterland. In 1963, the Commanding Officer of the Liberian National Guard was arrested on a charge of plotting to assassinate the President; ten years later an Assistant Minister of Defence, Prince Browne, and two lieutenant-colonels were charged with a similar plot against President Tolbert.[20] It is hard to tell how much substance there was to these allegations but it is understandable that the government should take them seriously, especially since the armed forces include a greater proportion of tribal Liberians than other central government institutions. In 1968, an assimilated Vai and former ambassador, Henry Farnbulleh, was imprisoned for attempting to mobilise tribal opinion against the government, allegedly with communist aid; he was released by President Tolbert in 1972.[21]

Tubman's sudden death in August 1971 produced none of the crises which had widely been predicted and Vice-President Tolbert took over remarkably smoothly, despite the rumoured attempts of a few members of the government to prevent him. After being Tubman's understudy for nearly twenty years,

Tolbert proved remarkably adept at establishing himself in power, creating a new style of administration without upsetting the balance of political forces on which post-war Liberian government had been based. He maintained Tubman's emphasis on unification, and recruited several hinterlanders to his administration, but added an appeal for self-help projects and national development far greater than the old President had shown. He also dispensed with some of the formality surrounding the Presidency, and allowed some liberalisation of political expression; since this has resulted in increased criticism of the President and his close associates, though, it is not clear how far it can be combined with what is still a highly elitist form of government. In foreign affairs, analogously, he continued Tubman's policy of maintaining friendly relations with other African states and a close connection with the USA, while seeking to establish a reputation of his own through tireless personal diplomacy. He joined most African states in breaking off relations with Israel in September 1973, and by early 1975 judged his reputation on the continent strong enough to risk inviting Mr Vorster of South Africa to Liberia. He also sought closer relations with Sierra Leone, expressed in the Mano River Declaration which provided for a customs union and other common activities, and which was signed by Presidents Tolbert and Stevens on the border between their two countries in October 1973.

POLITICAL DEVELOPMENTS SINCE 1945: SIERRA LEONE

Political developments in Sierra Leone over the same period have been vastly more eventful.[22] In January 1944, when Tubman came to power in Liberia, Sierra Leone was still governed as two largely separate units, the Colony and the Protectorate, under British colonial rule. The advisory Legislative Council did little to link the two, and African political mobilisation outside Freetown consisted only in a few small proto-political organisations among the chiefs and educated hinterlanders. The attempt to organise countrywide political parties dates only from the controversies over the 1951 constitution, which provided a majority of seats in the legislature for Africans, and – more importantly in local terms – gave the hinterland enough seats to outvote the Freetown peninsula. The resulting election was scarcely representative, since the Colony electorate was highly restricted and the Protectorate members were selected in a way which gave great influence to the chiefs, but the process helped to crystallise the division between Creoles and hinterlanders which prompted the formation of the first political parties: the National Council of the Colony of Sierra Leone for the Creoles, and the Sierra Leone People's Party (SLPP) for the hinterland. The National Council was doomed by the smallness of its electoral base, and the SLPP emerged as the dominant political party. Essentially conservative, it was based on an alliance between chiefs and educated hinterlanders, two groups who were closely related by family ties. Its leader, Dr Milton Margai, could call on support from both. Even so, it marked a decisive shift in political power away from the Creoles, in strong contrast to the entrenched position of the Americo-Liberians.

After 1951, it was thus clear that any opposition party had to draw support from the hinterland, either from rivalries within the very loose coalition of local elites which comprised the SLPP, or from a more populist appeal to groups excluded from it, or from the politicisation of ethnic rivalries within the hinterland. Despite the hostility towards chiefs, especially in the Northern Province, demonstrated by widespread rioting against chiefly corruption in 1955–6, the SLPP maintained its position in the 1957 elections, the first held under popular suffrage. The only party to try to capitalise on the legacy of the riots, the United Progressive Party (UPP), was too Creole-led to be effective, and gained only 5 of the 39 popularly elected seats. Of the remainder, 25 went to the SLPP, 8 to independents allied with it, and one to the Kono Progressive Movement (KPM), a party based on discontents in the diamond-mining Kono district. Within a short time of the election, disputes arose over Milton Margai's leadership of the party which led eventually to the secession of a group led by his younger brother Albert Margai and Albert's close associate Siaka Stevens; Albert Margai returned to the SLPP in 1960, but Siaka Stevens remained in opposition and formed the All People's Congress (APC), which became the main opposition party after independence in April 1961; a focus for discontents within the hinterland thus became available.

By independence, the initial Creole/Protectorate division had been bridged by the electoral supremacy of the Protectorate, the resulting realisation among Creoles they must join a hinterland-led political party to exert political influence, and the compensation provided by continuing Creole dominance of the civil service, the judiciary, and the professions. Subsequent political conflicts have therefore tended to be hinterland-based, involving the Creoles largely in a brokerage role. The most important conflicts at this time were those derived from the largely Mende and southern leadership of the SLPP – the Margais were Mende – and its elitist orientations. The APC was much more northern and also Freetown based, and its leader Siaka Stevens was a former trade unionist. In the 1962 elections it won 16 seats, all in the Northern Province and the former Colony, now called the Western Area; its ally the Sierra Leone Progressive Independence Movement (SLPIM) in Kono, successor to the KPM, won 4 more, against 28 for the SLPP and 14 independents. The fact that the independents and also the Paramount Chiefs (who held a further 12 seats) opted for the SLPP denied the APC any chance of forming a government, but it proved itself the most effective opposition which the SLPP had had to face.

After the election, Milton Margai had some success with a carrot-and-stick policy of offering inducements to opposition leaders to join the SLPP while restricting their local supporters. However, he died in office in April 1964, and the succession to the premiership of his brother Albert led to a very different situation. Firstly, Albert's defeat of the leading northern contender for the premiership, Dr John Karefa-Smart, intensified ethnic and regional conflict and led most northerners to look to the APC. Secondly, Albert's attempt to increase his power at the expense both of the opposition, and of other politicians in the loosely-knit SLPP, alienated a great deal of support and led eventually to his defeat in the election of March 1967. His proposals for a single-party state, for the declaration of a Republic, and for strengthening the SLPP's central machinery were all seen as attempts to improve his own position, and were widely opposed and eventually dropped. Likewise he tampered with the electoral machinery, but lacked the nerve to do so enough to ensure his own return. In the 1967 election the SLPP won 28 seats (including 6 rather dubiously opposed), almost all of the contested ones being in the Southern and Eastern Provinces; the APC won 32, including a virtually clean sweep of the Northern Province and Western Area, and two in Kono; and independents, mostly southerners opposed to Albert Margai, won six more. The Governor-General, a Creole, then invited Siaka Stevens to form a government; shortly after being sworn in, he was arrested by the Army Commander, Brigadier Lansana, at the behest of Albert Margai, and martial law was declared.

Lansana was ousted after two days by his middle-ranking officers, who formed a military regime under the National Reformation Council (NRC), and invited Lt Col Andrew Juxon-Smith to head it. The NRC governed for just over a year. It was displaced in April 1968 by a further coup led by NCOs, mostly of northern origin. These invited Stevens back from Guinea, where he had gone into exile, to lead a restored civilian regime. The APC under Stevens has retained power for the subsequent seven years, beating off challenges from the army, the SLPP, and opponents of Stevens within the Party. In the process, it has become increasingly authoritarian. The first major challenge, after the initial problems of restoring civilian rule, came from APC ministers opposed to Stevens' leadership, who broke away in September 1970 to form the United Democratic Party (UDP). In alliance with the SLPP, now a largely southern opposition party, this would have had considerable prospects of constitutionally displacing the government, and it was quickly banned. The discontents which had given rise to it stayed, and helped to prompt an abortive coup against Stevens in March 1971. Stevens brought in troops from neighbouring Guinea to support him, and in April 1971 had Sierra Leone declared a Republic with himself as President; the Army Commander implicated in the attempted coup was tried and executed.

During this time the SLPP had remained as the only legal opposition party; it retained appreciable support, especially in the south, and despite the leadership disputes left after Albert Margai's departure in 1967, it had hopes of gaining seats both in the north and in Freetown through its tacit alliance with the banned UDP. The general election of April 1973, however, was far more efficiently controlled than the 1967 one had been. In many areas, non-APC candidates were prevented from lodging their nominations; and every seat, with one trivial exception, went predictably to the APC. A bomb attack on the house of an APC politician in August 1974 was followed by the execution in July 1975 of several opposition leaders who were alleged to have instigated it, and in August 1975 the first steps were taken to turn Sierra Leone formally into the one-party state which it had already become in practice.

CHAPTER 3

RESOURCES

POLITICAL RESOURCES AND SOCIAL CLEAVAGE

Political resources derive from social cleavages which can be made relevant to competition for the benefits which the political system has to offer. In a totally homogeneous society, if such an impossible abstraction can be conceived, political competition would be reduced to a clash of personalities, which would themselves then become resources. In more differentiated situations, personalities are generally subordinated to competition between groups whose divisions are seen as being politically relevant. Votes, bribes, military coups and so forth are merely means by which these divisions are converted into a politically usable form. Similarly, political issues become important only in so far as they can be used to mobilise the distinctions between members of different and potentially rival groups; ideologies serve the same function in a rather more coherent and long-standing way, whether they be nationalist ones designed to sharpen the distinction between those within the political community and those outside it, or particularist ones designed to heighten the self-identity of internal competing groups.

For convenience of exposition, these cleavages – in Liberia and Sierra Leone as elsewhere – may be divided into two categories: vertical cleavages between groups which identify themselves, at least in some political contexts, as different; and horizontal ones between groups having varying access to status, wealth or power. The categories are obviously very closely connected, especially through relationships between communal identity and economic activity, and through the preferential access of some communities to special skills and the opportunities which these bring. Horizontal and vertical distinctions, too, divide into further forms of differentiation which may complement or displace one another, and each may be connected, especially in underdeveloped states, with resources external to the domestic society. For the moment, however, it is most convenient to look at the various resources one by one, and let their relationships emerge in due course.

VERTICAL CLEAVAGE

In both Liberia and Sierra Leone, communal identity is one of the most important factors shaping involvement in politics; but in both, though most markedly in Sierra Leone, there is no single form of this identity which overrides all others. Liberia may only with considerable reservations, and Sierra Leone scarcely at all, be described as a 'plural society' whose political life is determined by basic and non-cross-cutting ethnic conflicts.[1] Rather, different forms of cleavage arise in different contexts, and are brought into politics in different ways, depending on the divisions whose mobilisation is permissible under the operative rules, and on the prizes which these may be used to compete for. The main such cleavages are those between national and foreigner, between immigrant and indigenous communities, between different indigenous tribal groups, and between factions within the same community. Each of these will be considered in turn.

National and foreigner

The political role of the basic division between national and foreigner has been derived in Sierra Leone from the experience of colonialism, in Liberia from the maintenance of national integrity against encroaching colonial powers, and in both from the importance of foreign nationals in the modern economy. Despite the critical differences in *rules* derived from the presence or absence of colonialism, the sum of these influences on national identities in the two countries has been fairly similar.

Colonialism in Sierra Leone did not result in any articulate nationalism, in the sense either of hostility to the colonial power or of identity among the colonised. The colonial power was not, after the initial conquest, overtly repressive, and it established a working partnership with the Creoles in Freetown and the chiefs in the interior. Educational and economic development were not sufficient – by contrast with southern Ghana, for example – to provide the base for any radical nationalist political party, and the salience of the Creole/hinterland division during the critical period of initial politicisation cut off most of the would-be leaders of such a party from their potential supporters. A sense of national identity is more readily discernible in Liberia, where it has been fostered – at any rate among the politically conscious elite – by an awareness of Liberia's survival as the lone black African republic through the scramble for Africa and the League of Nations crisis of 1930. In neither case, however, has the sense of external threat been enough to make the maintenance of national unity or integrity a resource overriding cleavage within the domestic arena. In both, a legacy of division is derived from the very foundation of the state by settlers from outside, and this has inhibited the development of any active nationalist consciousness.[2]

The distinction between nationals and non-nationals in the domestic economy has provided a more productive field for generating political support. The role of foreigners in the economy – European, Asian and African – has already been referred to, and is not essentially different in the two countries. The politicisation of resentments against foreigners provides an attractive resource for politicians in power, since it emphasises linkages between governing groups and all sections of domestic society. Hence one finds President Tubman's son, Shad Tubman Jr, attacking foreign entrepreneurs during his period as President of the Liberian Congress of Industrial Organizations in the 1960s, precisely because this is a form of appeal which draws upon identities which he and ordinary trades unionists have in common, rather than on their considerable differences in terms of Liberian domestic cleavages.[3] Similar appeals have been used in attempts to bridge domestic conflict in Sierra Leone, especially by the Stevens government after 1968. Both countries have taken measures – to be considered in more detail later – to restrict foreigners in certain sectors of the economy, and both have nationality laws restricting Sierra Leone or Liberian citizenship to persons of Negro African descent.[4]

As against this, the external world can itself be considered, in some respects, as a resource. At its most diffuse, the Liberian government's need to establish good relations with its newly independent African neighbours has been one factor leading to increased participation for the hinterland. More specifically, the government's monopoly of control over official relations with the exterior gives it a powerful resource for domestic use. Economically, it gives access to revenues derived from trade, aid, and protection for foreign entrepreneurs. In the security field, as with Siaka Stevens' call for Guinean troops in 1971, it may provide forces which can be used to control domestic opponents. And in a symbolic way, the international recognition conferred by involvement in diplomatic activity can be used to reinforce the government's prestige and legitimacy in the domestic arena.

Immigrant and indigene

The most obvious and at any rate initially the most important source of internal political cleavage has been that between the descendants of the immigrant Creoles and Americo-Liberians, and those of the indigenous peoples. In the early history of the settlements it overrode all others, and in Liberia especially the symbolism of this period continues to be prominent. The coat of arms of the Republic, with its sailing ship symbol of immigration and its motto 'The Love of Liberty Brought Us Here', emphasises the connections between the government and the immigrant community, and many of its founding myths draw on the memory of warfare between the immigrants and local peoples. This warfare has continued into the present century, its last important manifestation being the Kru rebellion of the 1930s. In Sierra Leone, the colonial presence muted the connections between Creoles and government, but memories of hinterland hostility remain. The bitterest is that of the massacre of Creole traders and officials during the Hut Tax War of 1898, symbolising both the enmity between Creole and hinterlander and the abandonment of the Creoles by the colonial power to which they looked for protection. These symbols were mobilised during the later

1940s and early 1950s as part of an attempt to create a separatist Creole political movement.

Nonetheless, immigrant/indigene divisions have never hardened into the sharp cleavages produced, say, by European immigration into southern Africa. Connections between the two communities have existed since the early days. These include intermarriage, the common practice of adopting indigenous children into immigrant families, and the assimilation of hinterlanders through their association with the styles and institutions of the coast. Politically, too, the division has been muted, though differences in rules between the two countries have had an enormous and direct effect on the ways in which this has been done.

In Sierra Leone, the electoral rules introduced by the colonial government initially intensified the division between the Creole Colony and the tribal Protectorate. The 1951 elections were fought largely on this division. It could not long be used as an electoral resource, however, because of the disparity in voting strength between the two groups, and Creole participation in electoral politics has since taken the form of involvement in hinterland-led political parties. The Creole community retains interests in other areas of political competition, for example in maintaining its position in institutions such as the civil service and the judiciary. It retains also a conscious self-identity which has been intensified by threats to its position, first from the colonial government and more recently from the tribal element; communal institutions such as the masonic lodges have been used to defend its interests.[5] The basic issue in Creole/hinterland rivalry has nonetheless been settled by the shift in political power to the hinterland, and such elements of it as remain are no more than one among many issues in Sierra Leone politics.

In Liberia, the same division has been played down through the awareness of politically conscious Americo-Liberians, especially President Tubman, that the coastal community could not continue to vaunt its political supremacy without eventually prompting a disastrous hinterland reaction. The result has been a deliberate attempt to blur the distinction, though without substantially altering the existing rules which favour the immigrant community. The term 'Americo-Liberian' has fallen into disfavour, and symbols emphasising coast/hinterland divisions (such as the motto) have come under attack. The process by which educated hinterlanders took coastal names has been reversed with the adoption of indigenous names by coastal politicians. Much of this has been protective colouring, but some efforts have been made to associate hinterlanders with government both at the centre and, especially, in local administration. Membership of the coastal elite continues to operate as a powerful resource through the informal rules of patronage and family connection which still largely determine recruitment.

To an increasing extent coastal politicians find it useful to maintain some hinterland links, of family or more often of patronage, through which to extend their networks of political support. For a President, these links are essential, and both Tubman and Tolbert have used their hinterland 'farms' or estates as centres for the distribution of political and economic patronage and for symbolic association with the tribal peoples. Many other politicians have such estates, the functions of which are as much political as economic, and Senators like Charles B. Sherman in Cape Mount or Shad Tubman Jr in Maryland concern themselves as much with the tribal as with the immigrant element in their home counties.

Use of hinterland support as a resource *against* the coastal elite, on the other hand, continues to be actively prevented; this is the lesson of the Farnbulleh affair of 1968. Hence the immigrant/indigene cleavage has not been settled in Liberia to the same extent that it has in Sierra Leone. The maintenance of a rule structure based on the immigrant community's continued tenure of a favoured political position makes it necessary to adopt a strategy of assimilation and repression which – at least into the distant future – may always be reversed if any hinterland politician proves able to mobilise a resource base too great for the present rules to contain.

Tribe

Despite controversy over the appropriateness of the term 'tribe', there is no other word which describes so succinctly the identities which arise within African states from a combination of indigenous cultural patterns, colonial administrative practices, and competition for benefits in the modern sector. These identities exist both in Liberia and in Sierra Leone, and 'tribe' is, in common usage, the term used to describe them; nor, in general, is there any difficulty in discovering to which tribe any prominent hinterlander is held to belong. But 'tribe' is no fixed primordial attachment. It is, rather, a means of declaring an identity which may be founded as much on present goals as on ancestral descent. People of mixed parentage, or those who move away from their home area, have a good deal of latitude in choosing to which group they wish to be regarded as belonging; in Sierra Leone, the verb 'to declare' – as in 'he declared Temne' – is used to express what is, as much as anything, a matter of personal choice. In this respect, too, the boundaries between Creole or Americo-Liberian and hinterlander are as blurred as those between indigenous groups; Temne residents of Freetown may through society membership, intermarriage, religion and language become as Creole as their neighbours.[6]

Though in terms of social identity and local administration there is not much difference between a tribe in Liberia and in Sierra Leone, the political implications of tribe have been vastly different, again – as with the immigrant/indigene cleavage – because of the rule structures of the two countries. In Sierra Leone, the electoral supremacy of the hinterland, represented by the SLPP after its victory in 1951, left it open to challenge from the politicisation of divisions within the hinterland. These could draw on the SLPP's identification either with ruling elites within the hinterland as a whole, or with particular areas of it at the expense of others, and in fact did both. The area biases of the SLPP, which concern us here, arose initially almost coincidentally from the high proportion of its top leadership which came from Mendeland. Several factors reinforced this. Firstly, Milton Margai was a Mende. Secondly, most of the anti-chief disturbances of 1955–6, which helped to mobilise electoral support for opposition parties, were in the Temne north. Third, the splits and reunions in the SLPP in 1958–61 resulted in most of its Mende members returning to the fold, whereas many of the northern members remained in opposition under Siaka Stevens and the APC. The APC's successes in the north in the 1962 election further reduced the northern leadership of the SLPP, and when Albert Margai took over the Premiership in 1964 in preference to the Temne Dr John Karefa-Smart,[7] the SLPP's last chance of representing the entire hinterland disappeared. Mende rep-

Map B. Liberia and Sierra Leone: Administrative Boundaries. (Adapted from Gnielinski, Map 4, and Clarke, Map 10.)

resentation in the SLPP was reflected in the distribution of development funds to Mende areas of the country. Northern Temnes and Limbas, too, were most prone to migrate to cities and diamond areas where opposition to the SLPP was in any case greatest. The main diamond district, Kono, had grievances of its own which were naturally associated with the ethnic identity of the Kono people, and together these resources provided the base for a succession of Kono political movements.

Hence opposition politicians had an interest in mobilising tribal identities as resources for electoral support; even the SLPP did so once it went into opposition, appealing to Mende cultural symbols like the Poro Society in order to maintain a hold on its base in Mendeland. Politicians needed therefore to emphasise their own tribal identities, even when they scarcely had any. Siaka Stevens,

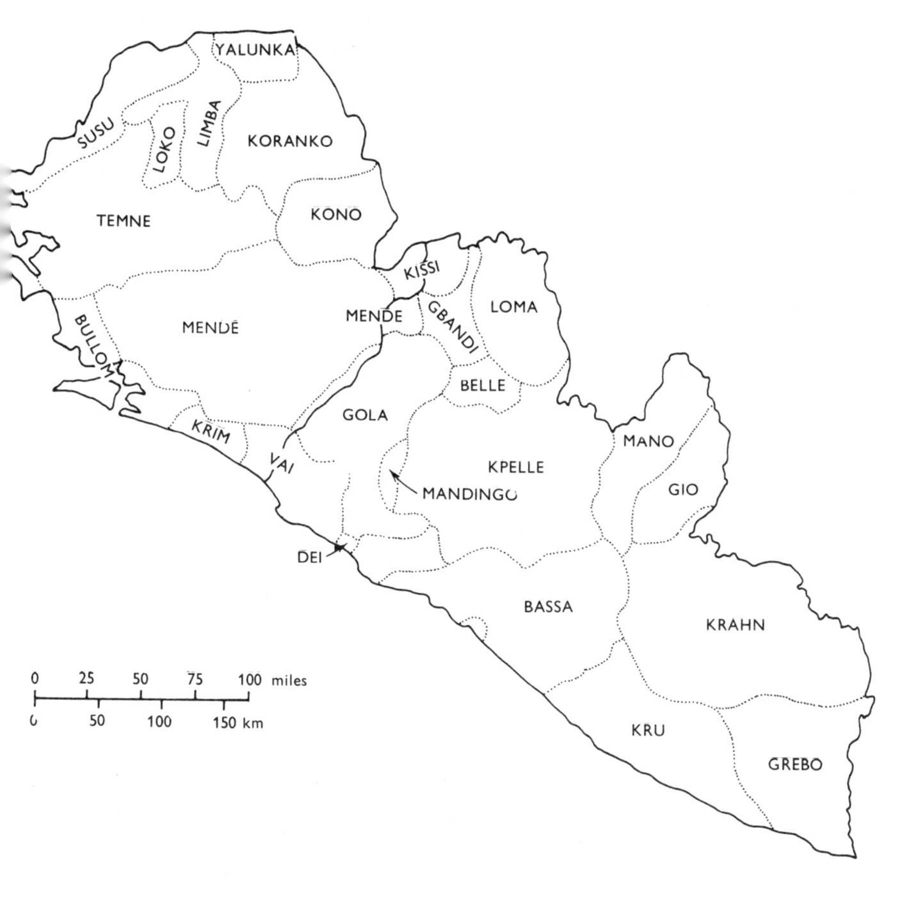

Map C. Liberia and Sierra Leone: Principal Tribal Groups. (Adapted from Gnielinski, Map 16, and Clarke, Maps 14 and 15.)

with a northern Limba father and a southern Gallinas mother, brought up in Mendeland, spending most of his life in Freetown, and married to a Temne, is the most thoroughly detribalised politician Sierra Leone has yet produced. Yet in the early 1960s he found it necessary to declare himself a Limba, in order to strengthen his claim to head a northern political party. In different circumstances in Sierra Leone, he might equally have 'declared' Mende. In Monrovia, he might have passed for an assimilated Americo-Liberian.

Though the political uses of tribe in Sierra Leone originated in the need to find bases for electoral competition, they soon spread into other areas. Albert Margai's use of Mendes in key administrative positions – Secretary to the Prime Minister, Establishment Secretary, Army Commander – extended them into the civil service. The National Reformation Council, despite its sweeping rhetorical attacks on tribalism, found it necessary to strike an ethnic and regional balance among its own members. Yet tribe has never become a resource to outweigh all others. Even in the electoral field, the SLPP at its lowest level of popular support retained leaders in the north and Kono who, had the electoral rules still been in force, might well have triumphed in the 1973 general election. The APC had a few Mende supporters even before 1967, and gained more when it had government patronage to distribute after 1968. Though important, tribal identity is no more than one resource among others.

In Liberia, it is not even that. Even though there are no tribes in Liberia with a proportion of the total population to match that held by both the Temne and Mende in Sierra Leone, it would not be difficult to conceive some broad lines of tribal division, for example between the north-western peoples – Vai, Kpelle, Loma – who share languages in the Mende group and an attachment to the Poro Society, and the south-eastern ones – Bassa, Kru, Grebo – who speak the Kru group of languages and do not use Poro. There would be nothing inevitable about such an alliance, and others could equally be imagined. But tribe has not been mobilised as a political resource, except to a very limited extent, because there has been no participant political structure within which to mobilise it. Such a structure, moreover, would first of all need to call in question the dominant role of the coastal elite, before hinterlanders gained sufficient control over political allocation to promote conflict over it among themselves.

Factional conflict

Much of the most intense conflict in both systems is based not on broad ethnic divisions but on factions whose opposing members share essentially similar origins and ambitions. The distinguishing feature of faction as a form of political cleavage is indeed precisely the fact that opponents are so close to one another in terms of the rules which they accept and the prizes which they seek that political conflict between them is reduced – and intensified – to a personal battle for rewards.

Faction is equally salient in both systems, and in both immigrant and indigenous communities, though the ways in which it is brought into political life to some extent vary with the rules in each country. Among the immigrants, it is most obvious in Liberia, largely because the Americo-Liberian community has much greater prizes to offer than has the Creole one; some of the forms which faction takes – through patronage links based on changing marriage alliances, for example – have been well described by Liebenow.[8] Faction within the Creole community is equally intense, though because of the competitive party system and their subordinate political position, many of the most overt conflicts have been about the extent to which and the terms on which Creoles should ally themselves with hinterland politicians. Few Creoles can have aroused such hostility within their own community as did two lawyers, Gershon Collier and Berthan Macaulay, through their alliance in 1964–7 with Albert Margai on terms which were seen as subverting the interests of the Creoles as a whole.

Conversely, faction among hinterland politicians is most obvious in Sierra Leone, because there hinterlanders come closer than in Liberia to the central allocation of power. Conflicts both within and between parties have as often been based on faction – perhaps with a little ideological flavouring – as on deep seated ethnic rivalry. The most striking case is Albert Margai's attempt to oust his brother Milton as leader of the SLPP in 1957, and his secession from the party the following year.[9] Similarly, the formation of the UDP in 1970 followed from the failure of a group of ministers, mostly Temne, to restrict the increasing power of Siaka Stevens within the APC. But faction in its purest form, in both Sierra Leone and Liberia, can be seen at chiefdom level, where broader sources of conflict are removed, and politics is concentrated almost exclusively on the struggle for office. Some of the factions which then arise, and the ways in which they are linked to national politics, will be described in the chapter on central–local relations.

HORIZONTAL CLEAVAGE

Whereas vertical cleavages define sources of identity which are useful in political life, horizontal cleavages define sources of opportunity. In Sierra Leone and Liberia, as in most underdeveloped countries, opportunities primarily depend on gaining access to a set of skills and institutions which in their essentials depend on imported technologies. Wealth, as has been shown, is for the most part created by the production, extraction or distribution of commodities which link West Africa to the economies of the industrial world. Status is conferred partly by position in indigenous hierarchies and value systems (themselves now adapted to the impact of the outside world), but equally by success in the new world of government and the professions. Power depends on the ability to control and manage a state administration, and hence at least to some extent on imported skills such as education or military training. The fact that an important group in the politics of each country comes from overseas and has a long association with the instruments of modernity helps to emphasise the importance of uneven opportunity: unequal opportunity is built into the socio-economic structure of Liberia and Sierra Leone, and the Creoles and Americo-Liberians are, so to speak, ex-officio beneficiaries of it.

Provided that the sources of stratification are recognised, it does not in my view matter very much whether the term used to describe it is 'elite' or 'class'. I prefer to speak of elites, since class implies assumptions of class consciousness and continuity, and the primacy of economic structure, which are best left open for investigation; there are nonetheless some forms of stratification for which class is the most appropriate term.[10] The term elite does not take so much for granted, and thus makes it easier to examine and compare aspects of stratification in the two countries. The openness of recruitment to elite positions may vary; so may the uses to which wealth, status and skills may be put in seeking political power; and so, most important of all, may the coherence and self-identity of the elite, and conversely the nature of the connections between those in elite positions and the rest. Coherence and self-identity largely turn on the ethnic homogeneity of the elite, and hence on the vertical cleavages already outlined. The role of other forms of stratification in defining opportunities for gaining political power will be discussed in the sections which follow.

Wealth and occupation

Though no figures for income distribution are available, there is no doubt that wealth is very unevenly allocated in both countries, or that those in high political office have a disproportionate share of it. The greater wealth of the Liberian economy, and the greater coherence of the Liberian elite, make both of these features more evident there than in Sierra Leone. But this does not make wealth an important source of political power, since it is generally political office which provides the opportunities for its acquisition, rather than the other way round. In other words, it enters the political arena more as a prize than as a resource. The fact that Liberian politicians, far more than Sierra Leonean ones, often run their own companies or take a prominent role in business is due to their long and undisturbed tenure of office, not to any special capacity to use their wealth to secure political allocations.

The main opportunities for producing wealth in the two economies, through trade or mineral exploitation, are in foreign hands except in so far as government action has brought them into indigenous ones. This has led to deliberate efforts by governments in both countries to divorce the main sources of production from the exercise of political power. Of course, governments ultimately depend on the foreign-managed economy and on the revenues which it generates; conversely, foreigners can and do use their wealth and control over key areas of the economy to protect themselves by discreet intervention in politics, using such means as bribery or support for political parties. Some of the resulting interactions will be considered in Chapter 7. But these interactions involve an exchange between separate though interdependent sources of economic and political power, rather than the simple control of one by the other. Liberian memories of Firestone's political influence during the 1920s and 1930s are sufficiently bitter to prompt resentment at any hint of company control, and one of the great achievements of Tubman's Open Door Policy in Liberian eyes has been to release the government from dependence on any single foreign company. In Sierra Leone, special legislation was passed just before the 1962 election to prevent Lebanese from standing for Parliament, because of the sitting members' fears that they might use their wealth to buy their way in.[11]

Paradoxically, the use of economic position as a political resource is more evident lower down the social and economic scale, among groups who otherwise would scarcely impinge on the political process at all, and for the most part these are concerned with appealing to government in order to protect their economic role, rather than with projecting representatives into political office. Trade unions are one example. Union membership is largely confined to the employees of foreign companies and a few state corporations. In Sierra Leone, they have provided some support for the APC, and Siaka Stevens made his way into politics initially as a union organiser in the iron-ore mines at Marampa; he is the only politician of any importance in either country to have risen from a union background. In Liberia, attempts have been made to bring unions under government control by appointing people closely associated with the government to head them; the sons of Presidents Tubman and Tolbert have successively been President of the Congress of Industrial Organizations, while the other central union congress, the Labour Congress of Liberia, was for many years headed by President Tubman's social secretary. Strikes have generally taken place in defiance of the union, and though labour organisations provide a potential resource, it is one which currently has few opportunities for political action.[12]

The only indigenous group in either country who are able to exercise effective political influence as a result of their role in the economy are the Kono diamond miners. These control a product which is not only valuable to the national economy, but which generates wealth in an easily cashable form for the people who actually produce it. They also have the numbers needed for electoral success and they have provided support for representatives either within the APC or in a succession of local political parties.[13] By contrast, and unlike some other West African countries such as Ghana and Senegal, cash crop producers have not been sufficiently numerous or important to the national economy to provide any major source of political support.

Status and skills

Status is rather more subtly related than wealth to the exercise of political power, and it is correspondingly more difficult to disentangle the ways in which it serves as a resource from those in which it serves simply as a prize. Political office brings respect with it, and high status is correspondingly conferred, at least publicly, on those groups and individuals who secure office and on the social institutions through which they do so. At the same time, status and educational skills provide a partly independent source of political and economic opportunity. But though the causal connections between status and office are intricate, it is possible to sketch out some of the sources of status in the two countries, and to relate them to their differing distributions of political power.

In Liberia, the Americo-Liberian core constitutes a status group outweighing any source of status derived from the hinterland. Membership of a prominent chiefly family may confer status within one's hinterland group, especially among peoples such as the Vai for whom descent is an important qualification for chieftaincy. But even this source of status, which is scarcely cashable in national terms, is reduced in Liberia by the absence of the rules which in Sierra Leone restrict chieftaincy to members of specified chiefly families. Status and membership of the central core therefore very largely coincide; status is conferred on hinterlanders, even if they retain their ethnic identities, by their capacity to make their way up within the institutions of the centre. In its most diffuse form, this status is coterminous with the distinctive Liberian word 'kwi', which may most closely be rendered as 'civilised'. To be kwi is above all to be educated, and to move in the world of western tastes, motor travel and the English language which distinguishes the kwi from the 'country people', and qualifies them for salaried employment.[14] Being kwi, rather than being ethnically Americo-Liberian, is the essential condition for participation in the political system. Within the core, hinterlanders acquire status as they gain the positions which the centre has to offer, as generals, ministers, county superintendents, members of masonic lodges, or by marriage into a prominent family. For members of the Americo-Liberian community too, political position and the status derived from family or institutional membership are too closely connected to make it possible or even very profitable to determine which is the cause of the other.

The position of the Sierra Leonean Paramount Chief and chiefly family provides by contrast a source of status which is diffused throughout the hinterland and has been enormously important as a resource for the recruitment of national politicians. The British legacy of indirect rule not only gave the chief a rather more prestigious position than his Liberian equivalent. When coupled with the exclusion of the Creoles from both land ownership and administrative office in the Protectorate, it also made the chief – rather than the Americo-Liberian politician with his hinterland estate – the most suitably placed intermediary between local politics and the central political system. The role of the chief in local administration, with the general lack of mobilisation of social and economic issues, has helped to make chieftaincy the most coveted prize in local politics and to create factions within chiefdoms based on support for rival chiefly families.

Members of these families have thus gained a local political following which they could use to mobilise electoral support, which in turn enabled them to acquire a place in central politics.

This base has been supplemented by special access to modern educational skills, which in both Sierra Leone and Liberia have tended – initially at least – to reinforce rather than challenge the existing distribution of status and political power. Bo School, the first and for many years the only secondary school in the Protectorate, was founded explicitly for the sons and nominees of chiefs, and many of the early hinterland leaders, including Milton Margai, were educated there. The resulting awareness of the value of formal education, and the fact that members of chiefly families have been more likely than others to possess the financial means to pay for it, has perpetuated this link. Several writers have clearly demonstrated the importance of this combination of educational qualifications and chiefly connections in the hinterland political leadership, especially in the SLPP.[15] Even the APC has included an appreciable proportion of members of chiefly families, and this number increased after 1968 when the party sought to extend its support by recruiting established politicians from the south.

Education has also helped to sustain the position of both Creoles and Americo-Liberians. Both communities have a long educational tradition. Fourah Bay College in Freetown was founded in 1827, and Liberia College, now the University of Liberia, in 1862. Until the last two decades, entry to these institutions has largely been restricted to members of the immigrant community, and has provided them with an enormous superiority in the possession of professional skills.[16] In Liberia, this has strengthened the political structure; in Sierra Leone, as already noted, it has helped to compensate the Creoles for the loss of political supremacy.

The rapid expansion of education in both countries during the last two decades, and especially its extension to the hinterland, is bound to have a more disruptive effect by placing an important resource – and one strongly linked to political and economic expectations – in the hands of groups hitherto largely excluded from power. In Sierra Leone, this provided one source of support for the APC. In Liberia, where it is implicitly more hostile to the existing political structure, its effects have so far been mitigated by recruiting educated hinterlanders to posts both in the central government and in the county administrations. However, Liberian university students now come mostly from the hinterland, and are generally hostile to the government.[17] The extension of primary education in the hinterland provides them with a potential constituency which is likely to prove increasingly difficult to contain within the political structure.

But if status can provide a political resource, so in a sense can its opposite. In Sierra Leone, hostility towards status holders has generally been directed against Paramount Chiefs, whose illegal exactions have been a constant source of complaint, occasionally breaking out in violence. The clearest case was the rioting in the Northern Province in 1955–6, and several opposition parties sought to mobilise the discontents which these disturbances revealed, most importantly – come the 1962 election – the APC.[18] Similarly in Kono, the wealthy Paramount Chiefs who had made their fortunes from diamonds tended to support the SLPP, and these were opposed by the political movements – the KPM and SLPIM, and ultimately the APC – which drew their strength from grievances among illicit diamond miners.[19] In Liberia, since status is implicitly linked with the Americo-Liberian community and the governing elite, so is any populist feeling implicitly hostile to the existing political system; its political manifestations are therefore suppressed.[20]

The structures of control

Although the control of government organisations is the main prize which political competition has to offer, it can be regarded as a resource in the sense that, once achieved, it can be used to perpetuate its holder's tenure of power, and to offset many of the resources which may be controlled by his opponents. On the other hand, it is very difficult to distinguish this resource either from the rules in operation in a particular place and time, since these determine the form of governmental structures and the ways in which they can be used, or from other resources, since these are likely to be implicit in the composition of the government and the measures which it takes to curb its rivals. Only occasionally does a government act solely as a government, without reference to the social cleavages which define its supporters and opponents. In Liberia, for instance, the regime is so closely connected with the social structures of the central elite that the resources of government in itself are almost impossible to disentangle.

It is easy enough, however, to sketch the forms which governmental resources take. They derive firstly from the control of coercion, and secondly from the opportunity to extract financial resources from the economy and redistribute them in the form of patronage and other personal rewards. In both countries, the government is the most important source of wealth and highly paid employment, though the Liberian government, with expenditure of $39 per head of population in 1970 against $15 for Sierra Leone, is by this measure more strongly placed.[21] The respective censuses of 1962 and 1963 also show Liberia as having a markedly higher proportion of her active population employed in government services (6.0% against 3.1% for Sierra Leone), with smaller percentages than Sierra Leone in mining, commerce and manufacturing.[22] Though one may infer from this that employment opportunities outside government are greater in Sierra Leone, there are plenty of Sierra Leonean cases to show the importance of patronage in helping the incumbent government to stay in power.[23]

One measure of the relative importance in Sierra Leone of governmental controls against the resources implicit in popular support is provided by the role of government in elections. This has increased steadily in the three post-independence elections of 1962, 1967 and 1973. The 1962 elections appear on the whole to have been fairly conducted, and the opposition parties were able to campaign reasonably freely, apart from some harassment at the local level; the resources of government were here chiefly exercised through the patronage inducements which the SLPP was able to offer its opponents and independents after the election, and through its ability to control Paramount Chiefs who were at the same time Members of Parliament and government administrative agents. In 1967, a more determined attempt to control the election was made, by securing the unopposed return of six SLPP members, and by a certain amount of ballot-rigging, but this was not enough to prevent the opposition APC from winning; it was only after this failure to rig the election that Albert Margai tried to make a straightforward use of coercive resources by bringing in the army, a move which – though successful in leading to a year of military rule – was fatal to his own position. The APC in 1973 made no such mistake, and by the use of the coercive machinery at its disposal prevented the opposition in most areas from filing nominations at all. In Liberia, the government has never permitted its opponents to organise popular support, and few of them have been foolhardy enough to attempt to do so.

Military intervention in politics is a less reliable indicator of the importance of governmental controls, partly because a civilian regime may be as coercive as a military one, and partly because military intervention may be generated by other conflicts – ethnic ones, for instance – rather than by the concerns of the military as such. To some extent, however, the army's ability to gain political power may reflect the strength of coercive resources against other sources of political influence which between them give legitimacy to a civilian regime. The Sierra Leone coup of 1967, ousting a party which had just won a majority in a general election, is a particularly clear case of this.

The structures of control, of course, are not important only at the central level. The threat of coercion and the promise of economic reward, both emanating from the centre, are among the most powerful resources at work in local politics, and a Paramount Chief, backed by the County Superintendent or the District Officer, may use his powers as a government agent to override or counterbalance resources generated, say, by local traditional rivalries or attachments. This is most evident in Liberia, where the hinterland administration is more obviously alien and imposed; in Sierra Leone, the legacy of indirect rule helps to associate government with an established social order, and it is difficult to distinguish clearly a chief's governmental role from his role as leader of the local community. In this respect, the local situation is the reverse of that at the centre, where it is in Liberia that social structure and governmental power are most closely enmeshed.

Though it has been necessary to anticipate some of the differences in rules between Liberia and Sierra Leone in order to compare the aspects of their social structures which are most relevant to political conflict, these structures in themselves do not substantially differ. Despite a few variations, the sources of social identity and of wealth, status and power are much the same in the two countries. Such differences between them as have emerged have been due not so much to the social resources in themselves as to the rules through which they have been mobilised. These rules, rather than anything inherent in the social structures of the two countries, have been the most important factor influencing the openness of recruitment to elite positions, and hence the homogeneity of the elite and the connections between vertical and horizontal forms of social cleavage. The rules themselves now need more detailed examination.

CHAPTER 4

RULES

RULES AND SOCIAL EXPLANATION

Politics, in common with other social sciences, has to find some way to explain actions, without recourse to the general causal laws which apply at least in some of the natural sciences, but which are excluded from social science explanation by human free will (and hence unpredictability), and by the complexity of social situations. At the same time, human actions do in fact display a fair degree of regularity, and so it is tempting to seek to explain them by using some concept which attempts to order the no-man's land between causal law explanation on the one hand, and random behaviour on the other. This is where 'rules' come in; but since there is little agreement as to what the term should mean or how it should be used, I must offer my own interpretation before going further.[1]

Rules, as I use the word, are a means of indicating the constraints on political behaviour. Politicians are not free to do as they will in their pursuit of prizes, even if the resources at their disposal are fixed. They are limited, partly by the legal requirements of the system in which they operate, partly by moral norms and expectations, and partly by their own estimates of what is prudent, or worth risking, in the situation at hand. All of these factors constitute rules, which between them order the operating environment of the politician. They establish the prizes which the system has to offer, indicate the means by which these can be competed for, and hence favour or disfavour the particular skills and resources at a politician's command.

Even this brief outline suggests a number of different kinds of rule, or different usages of the term, which to some extent require separate treatment. First, it is possible to distinguish *formal rules*, which specify legal constitutional and administrative structures and procedures. These constitute the public framework within which the system is deemed to operate, and in principle at least they should be clearly set out and legally enforced; they are rules in the commonest everyday use of the word. Secondly, there are those varied codes or practice which I lump together under the general heading of *informal rules*. These are customary (but not legally specified) political practices, whether normatively affirmed by political actors (normative rules), or merely practically available to them on a sufficiently regular basis to enter into their conception of the political environment within which they select their actions (pragmatic rules); they are rules of personal action rather than of public principle, though they will obviously be guided by the attitudes prevalent in the society. Thirdly, it is possible to refer to the ***rule structure***, or set of rules, to indicate the collection of rules of all kinds which coexist within a given polity at a particular time.

None of these kinds of rule, it must be emphasised, actually *determine* behaviour. Formal rules may be (and often are) broken by politicians who believe that they can get away with it, or they may be changed by those who have the power. Normative rules may be openly flouted or covertly evaded. Merely prudential rules cannot be broken in the same sense, but since they depend in part on the judgement of fallible actors, they cannot be used as an external yardstick to which these actors' behaviour must conform. The rule structure, being a codification of existing rules, simply changes with any change in its constituent parts.

The sense in which rules explain behaviour is not so much legal as ecological. Since rules indicate constraints, they equally provide a means of understanding the behaviour of those who act within these constraints. Actors who fail to abide by the rules are unlikely to survive, though occasionally these may throw up a mutant – to carry the analogy further – who proves better adapted to a changing world than his fellows who continue in the conventional way, and in this case the rule structure will change to accommodate him. In a similarly ecological vein, the rule structure provides niches into which some kinds of politician – those with particular resources, who act in particular ways – may comfortably fit, while denying protection to other kinds; it thus helps to explain why actors of a given type – army officers, say, or Paramount Chiefs – are more successful in some political systems than others. The rule structure also helps to explain the behaviour of politicians who seek to adapt themselves to the currently (or in their judgement prospectively) favoured mode of action, say by crossing to the governing party or joining the opposition, or by seeking to build a tribal base, or by joining the army.

The strength of these ecological influences, and hence their capacity to explain behaviour, depends firstly on the extent to which the actors can change the rules, and secondly on the uncertainty or inconsistency of the rule structure at any given time. A rule which you can change does not influence your behaviour in the same way as one which is for practical purposes fixed and immutable, though rule changing may have costs as well as benefits which need to be taken into account. Governments may adapt to their own advantage the environment within which they and other politicians have to act, in the same way that human beings may adapt the environment of themselves and other living creatures. In either case, short-term advantage may not be long-term wisdom. The legislation which locks up your opponents may breed the reaction which ousts you from power. For the opponents, it constitutes a new formal rule to which they must adapt if they are not to go under. But for the government it is scarcely a rule at all; it has escaped from some constraints on its actions, even though in doing so it must eventually run into others. Uncertainty likewise diminishes the effectiveness of rules, since a rule structure which is taken for granted limits the perceived range of possible actions more than one which in the actors' view may presently change. Even if you are in no position to change it yourself – by launching a coup, for instance – you may need to take account of the possibility that someone else may do so.

Rule inconsistency is a somewhat trickier concept. Formal rules generally embody some machinery for resolving apparent contradictions. Normative rules may certainly be inconsistent with one another, especially when different groups hold conflicting expectations as to how an actor – a Paramount Chief, for example – ought to behave; the actor may himself be torn by these conflicts, but in order to survive he will have to adapt himself to them pragmatically as best he may. The problems arise at the level of pragmatic rules, and of the rule structure as a whole. For a particular actor, there is at any given time only one best course of action (whatever the difficulties of calculating what this is), but the pragmatic rules followed by one set of actors may clash to a greater or lesser extent with those followed by others, with consequences for political stability. An incongruence equally arises in the rule structure when the formal rules do not closely correspond with the informal ones: when there are few constraints on breaking the formal rules, which thus do not provide much guide as to what one can actually get away with. In this case, the formal rules are likely either to be displaced, or else to be covertly adapted to the needs of those actors whose resources are pragmatically most important.

This digression into the concept of political rules may be seen to require some apology. In fact, the issues which it raises are constantly relevant to the politics of Liberia and Sierra Leone, and especially to the variations in rules which are important in explaining the differences between them. These variations now call for attention.

FORMAL RULES

Political scientists during the last twenty years have tended to discount the importance of formal rules, linking them with the legalistic constitutionalism of the early years of the discipline. In post-colonial Africa, the rapid displacement of constitutions has led to a further downgrading of their status, and resulted in political analyses which largely disregard them. Process – how men behave – has been seen as more significant than structure – how the state is regulated. Nonetheless formal rules serve useful functions in political comparison. Those of them which are beyond a political actor's immediate control help to shape his actions, and can thus be used – by the observer – in explaining why actors with similar resources should behave in different ways; and even those rules which governments in power shape for themselves can be used to indicate, though not to explain, the ways in which such governments perceive their position and the resources on which they rely. Provided that they are adequately integrated with the forces or resources which act through them, formal rules therefore deserve rather more attention than they have frequently received.

First and most importantly, formal rules define the national boundaries of Liberia and Sierra Leone. They thus determine the applicability of every other rule to people within one system and the other, and establish the distinction between citizen and foreigner. The fact that these boundaries have scarcely been challenged, despite their initial artificiality and the arbitrariness with which they divide communities between different countries, indicates the effectiveness of at least some formal rules in channelling political activity.

Secondly, formal rules determine the prizes, and more particularly the offices, which are available in the political system, and in principle at least they specify the ways in which these are related to one another and the means by which they are obtained. In Liberia, the main ones have been constant throughout the period under discussion, except for the changes in local government in the hinterland instituted in 1963–4. In Sierra Leone, there have been three principal sets of rules, though the shifts between them have left many aspects of the rule structure undisturbed. The first constitution remained in effect from Independence in April 1961 until March 1967, and from April 1968 until April 1971; the National Reformation Council ruled by decree from March 1967 until April 1968; and the Republican Constitution has been in force since April 1971. Transitional arrangements operating for a few days apiece in 1967, 1968 and 1971 may be disregarded.[2]

The principal prize to be allocated in each system is that of central political control, which as in most countries may be equated with the offices which carry with them the right to direct the national executive. In Sierra Leone, this has been vested in the Governor-General, Prime Minister and Cabinet under the Independence Constitution, and in the President, Prime Minister and Cabinet under the Republican one; the Prime Minister in the latter held the office of Vice-President until the two roles were separated in 1975. Before 1971 the Prime Minister's power to appoint other ministers effectively ensured his supremacy within the Cabinet, which in turn had the power to displace the Governor-General. Since then, the dominant position in the central executive, in practice rather than by formal constitutional ruling, has been held by the President. Between 1967 and 1968, essentially the same prize was vested in the eight-man National Reformation Council, under its Chairman. In Liberia, this prize has throughout been held by the President, whose Cabinet officers and other executive officials are directly appointed by him. Most Cabinet members head executive ministries, though in Sierra Leone a few Paramount Chief Representatives are customarily brought into the Cabinet as Ministers without Portfolio.

In Sierra Leone, the Governor-General was until 1971 nominated by the Cabinet; since then, the President has been chosen by the House of Representatives, though not a member of it. He selects as Prime Minister a Representative who can command a majority in the House; Ministers also must be Representatives.

The House of Representatives, and through it the Parliamentary Constituency, have thus been the formal (and to some extent actual) arena in which the prize of central political control has been allocated. The Liberian President and Vice-President are formally elected by popular vote for an eight-year term, followed if re-elected by subsequent four-year terms.[3] The franchise has been extended from the descendants of the original settlers to include all adult citizens, though in the absence of party competition this is more formal than effective. If the President resigns or dies in office the Vice-President succeeds to the Presidency, as Tolbert did in 1971; if the Vice-President also resigns, as happened in 1930, the Secretary of State/Minister of Foreign Affairs takes over.[4] Unlike Sierra Leone, members of the legislature have no formal say in the selection of the executive, and are excluded from ministerial office.

The Sierra Leonean legislature has only a single chamber, the House of Representatives, to which elections based on single-member constituencies are held at five-yearly intervals. The number of ordinary members has increased at each post-independence election, from 62 in 1962 to 66 in 1967 and 85 in 1973, the last election being held a year late to make up for the year lost under the NRC, which suspended the legislature. In addition, the Chiefdom Councillors in each of the twelve Districts elect one Paramount Chief from their own District, who then becomes a member of the House with the same status as other Representatives, though Paramount Chief Representatives customarily do not belong to any political party. Since 1974, the President has had the power to co-opt up to three additional MPs, and has used it to appoint army and police chiefs to Parliament. The Liberian legislature has two chambers: a Senate, with two Senators elected for four-year terms from each of the nine Counties; and a House of Representatives, currently of sixty members elected for two-year terms, with between four and ten from each County and one additional Representative for each of the five separately administered Territories. Unlike Sierra Leone, there are no demarcated single-member constituencies, and Representatives are chosen for the County as a whole.

Of the supplementary structures of central government, the most important in both countries are the civil bureaucracy, the judiciary, and the army. At the formal level, some differences exist in the rules governing these structures, especially the bureaucracy. In Liberia, where all executive appointments are at the President's disposal, there is no formal distinction between political and non-political appointments, nor is there any formal provision for recruitment and promotion within government departments. Appointments are made directly by the President of particular individuals to particular posts, a practice which provides enormous opportunities for presidential patronage. In Sierra Leone, a distinction exists between political appointments, of Ministers and Parliamentary Secretaries, and civil service ones which comprise the remainder. Civil service appointments are made by the Public Service Commission, which is nominally independent of the government of the day, except for the most senior officials –

of Permanent Secretary rank – who are appointed by the Governor-General or President. Similarly, judicial officers in Sierra Leone are appointed by a Judicial Service Commission, whereas in Liberia they are appointed by the President subject to the approval of the Senate. Control of the Armed Forces is in both countries formally vested in the President as Commander-in-Chief, with day-to-day control under a Minister of Defence. In Sierra Leone, Siaka Stevens held the Defence portfolio both as Prime Minister and, after April 1971, as President.

The rules covering local administration in both countries provide for an administrative hierarchy extending down from the centre to the Province, District and Chiefdom in Sierra Leone, and the County, District and Chiefdom in Liberia, in each case with a few anomalous jurisdictions. They also provide for the appointment of local officials and the selection of local representatives at the centre. Since these rules, and the various changes in them, are intimately connected with central–local relations, they will be examined in greater detail in the chapter on Centre and Periphery.

Within the boundaries of the state, the formal rules thus establish a hierarchy of offices which provide both a mechanism for government and a prize for political competition. But though the hierarchy itself can largely be defined by formal rules alone, the allocation of offices within it is heavily influenced by informal conventions and practices which modify or displace the formal ones, with the result that in the critical area of political conflict the two kinds of rule can scarcely be considered separately.

INFORMAL RULES

Informal rules, the collections of social attitudes and institutions which affect the ways in which the formal ones actually operate, are both pervasive and difficult to codify. They are nonetheless critical in explaining how it is that resources ostensibly similar can be incorporated in politics in very different ways. The first and in many ways the most important difference between the two countries is in the reference groups which set these rules, though these groups of course tend to reflect the existing distribution of power. The relationships between the groups which hold power, the rules which they set, and the resources on which they rely are too close to be satisfactorily disentangled.

In Liberia, the principal referent has remained constant in the Americo-Liberian community. This has needed to adapt itself to the demands of subordinate groups in the economy and the hinterland, but it has continued to set the rules within which this adaptation has taken place, and it has passed on to other politicians many of its own assumptions and practices about the exercise of power. In Sierra Leone, an equivalent position was initially held by the colonial government, which established the original formal rules of the system and enforced them on the various indigenous actors. It stood at the head of a conglomerate polity, comprising Creoles in Freetown and the professions, chiefly families in local administration, alien traders and companies, and other groups, which fitted together beneath an imposed colonial authority and devised their own informal rules within the colonial system.

There is no need to ascribe this to the Machiavellian practices of colonial divide-and-rule: the colonial government's mere presence helped to ensure it, and a very deliberate strategy would have been needed to ensure any other result. What is important is that different sets of informal rules emerged, both from the internal organisation of the communities, and from their differing and changing relationships with the administrative structure. The colonial withdrawal removed the main source of coherence, and made it necessary for the groups which were left behind to reformulate their relationships with one another. The rules, formal and informal, are still being adapted to this changed situation.

The clearest example is the way in which colonial rule insulated the Creoles from the hinterland and vice-versa. The Creoles, despite their high educational and managerial attainments, were prevented from establishing any appreciable linkages with the hinterland either administratively, since the key posts were until very shortly before independence in the hands of the British officials, or economically, since they were prohibited from owning land in the Protectorate and their early trading networks were ousted by alien competition. Within their own community, they developed institutions similar to those of the Americo-Liberians, though in an attenuated form due to their much slighter access to political power. The extended family, the Churches and the Freemasons are still in evidence,[5] as are the attitudes derived from their professional skills and identification with the colonial regime. In the Protectorate, the Paramount Chiefs and their families received appreciable local advantages, both political and economic, but lacked until the 1950s any mechanism through which these could be turned to advantage in the central administration. The informal rules which they devised were concerned with essentially local issues: with chiefdom conflicts and, especially in the South, with communal regulation through the 'secret societies' – the freemasonries, in effect – known as the Poro.[6]

In addition, the colonial rules which did ultimately link the actors in Sierra Leone politics with one another were themselves ambivalent, and this ambivalence has carried over into the politics of the independent state. On the one hand, indigenous governments inherited the centralising legacy of colonialism. Habits of deference to the central government continued, and were strengthened both by the coercive supremacy of the centre and by the central allocation of funds. As against that, the formal electoral rules established by the colonial government as a means of creating a national political structure were implicitly decentralising in their emphasis on votes, and several features of Sierra Leone society combined to make this legacy also a much more enduring one than in most ex-colonial African states. No nationalist party with the monopolist capabilities of the Guinean PDG or the Ghanaian CPP emerged to transform the ballot box into an instrument of central control, and the conciliatory style of the first Prime Minister, Milton Margai, was far from that of Sekou Touré or Nkrumah. Instead, local factionalism and chiefly oligarchy helped for a time at least to make elections an instrument for local influence, and ethnic rivalry at the national level was not so great as to make the resulting party competition intolerable.[7] The Creoles, with their professional skills and attachment to metropolitan values, found in the maintenance of electoral rules a means to sustain their role in the system and the autonomy of those parts of it, such as the judiciary and the civil service, in which they were well entrenched. Thus, no institution or set of actors capable of reintegrating the varied elements in Sierra Leone politics into a single coherent rule structure has yet emerged, a point which the army's incursion into politics and subsequent failure to establish itself there only helps to emphasise. Some of the implications of this fact for Sierra Leone politics and the role of rules in them will be examined in the next section.

In Liberia, informal rules largely concern the internal dynamics of the elite. Though this community is highly factionalised, in the sense that intense rivalries exist between individuals and groups within it, it possesses common and accepted mechanisms which give coherence to the community as a whole. The family, with its numerous ramifications and connections, provides the basic unit for political patronage, and for the extension of alliances with other family groups. Liebenow has elegantly mapped out some of the major family networks, and shown how the appointment of a leading family member to an important post is followed by the promotion of his relatives to subordinate positions.[8] Equally, a major politician's decline is accompanied by his protégés' failure to maintain their posts, and a divorce may signify the ending of a connection between family groups, just as a marriage indicates their alliance. At a higher level, the community is linked by membership of an enormous collection of voluntary organisations, advancement in which increases one's status and access to useful contacts. These include churches, the Episcopalian Church generally holding the most prestigious position, though President Tolbert is Baptist; charitable organisations such as the YMCA; friendly societies such as the United Brothers of Friendship or the United Order of Odd Fellows; and clubs with such names as Triple Six or Crowd 18. Two institutions have some claim to rank in the Americo-Liberian community as a whole: the Freemasons, by far the most important of the friendly societies, to which virtually all leading coastal politicians belong; and the True Whig Party.

These institutions transform entirely a nominally open rule structure into one dependent on central co-option. Not since the 1870s has any effective multi-party system existed in Liberia, and even that, confined to the coastal settlements, scarcely challenged the centralised nature of political allocation. Since then the True Whig Party, through its close connections with other core institutions, has been able to control admission to political office, and ensure that its candidates give due support to the principles of patronage on which it is based.

These rules do not restrict recruitment entirely to the coastal core, and in this respect especially they have been adapted over the last two decades. It has always been possible for hinterlanders in small numbers to assimilate themselves to the Americo-Liberian community, especially through intermarriage and adoption, and to work their way up within it in such a way that they become almost indistinguishable from its original members. Recently, as this slow process has become inadequate to incorporate resources arising in the hinterland, hinterlanders have increasingly been co-opted into government, though generally without receiving a base either in its associated coastal institutions or, more importantly, in their own home areas. This process will be looked at in the section on political recruitment. The system gains further flexibility through conventions of local self-government, initially in the coastal counties alone, which were extended to the hinterland by the local government reforms of 1963–4. Political activity outside the rules set by the core is not permitted, and its manifestations are suppressed.

In Liberia, formal rules reflect the distribution of power, but have little allocative capacity independent of the social structure within which they are set. Occasionally, as with Tolbert's constitutional succession on Tubman's death, they may be important within this structure. Formal rules are thus maintained. The formalities of nominations and electoral campaigning, for example, are meticulously adhered to: but this is precisely because the transactions performed through these rules are scarcely open to dispute. Thus formal rules in Sierra Leone, because they did not simply reflect the hegemony of any particular group, but rather provided a framework for competition between groups, have proved initially more important but subsequently less enduring than the Liberian ones. The informal rules which initially restricted government have declined, but have not been replaced by any new set of informal rules which – as in Liberia – tie in the operations of government with the attitudes and institutions of a dominant section of the society.

RULES AND THE MOBILISATION OF RESOURCES

Since in Sierra Leone the constitutional rules were initially imposed by the colonial regime, and were beyond the immediate control of local politicians, it was there that such rules had the greatest independent effect in allocating political power. This is especially clear when one looks at the arrangements for the 1951 and 1957 elections, and at the resource-holders which these arrangements favoured. The electoral rules themselves helped to give salience to vertical lines of cleavage, as is almost universally the case where communal identities outweigh awareness of class or elite/mass distinctions, and where horizontal communications between sub-elite groups in different areas are poorly developed. Under these conditions, feelings of communal solidarity help to reinforce the hold which those already in elite positions have over their fellows, since they are in the best position to compete for the available prizes while presenting themselves as the representatives of the community as a whole. In rural Sierra Leone, despite the dissatisfactions with chiefly power evidenced by the 1955 riots, the holders of high status, i.e. chiefly, resources were able to strengthen their access to the new electoral prizes in two main ways. Firstly, as the local agents of government, they could take administrative or judicial action against opponents, under some such pretext as that these had failed to show due respect to the Paramount Chief. Secondly, the detailed rules for the elections, especially in 1951, heavily favoured the chiefs; in 1951, the hinterland members of the Legislative Council were indirectly elected by the District Councils and the Protectorate Assembly, on both of which the chiefs were strongly represented. In the 1956 constitutional reforms, the chiefs were guaranteed 12 seats in the 57-seat legislature, and the constituencies for the popularly elected seats were divided along chiefdom boundaries and facilitated political organisation through the chiefdom.

The chiefs, however, were too closely tied to the local arenas and to administrative dependence on the government to be able to seek the main prizes, which were at the centre. The greatest gainers from the new electoral system were those who, combining local electoral strength with the educational backing needed to manage politics at the centre, were able to make the necessary shift between the two levels of political activity. The preferential access of chiefly nominees to modern education, already referred to, meant that the families and protégés of chiefs were especially favoured. Of the 25 hinterland representatives elected in 1957, 16 belonged to chiefly families; in the 1962 elections the proportion was even greater, since just over 80% of the successful hinterland candidates were related to paramount chiefs and other traditional authorities.[9] However, other local men such as traders or teachers who possessed secondary schooling were able to win elections despite not belonging to chiefly families, especially in the North and Kono where opposition to the chiefs was greatest.[10]

The lines of cleavage which determined the ways in which these holders of electoral resources competed or combined with one another depended largely on the nature of the prizes available at different levels. At a national level, the major parties were concerned mostly with winning control of the executive government, and this prompted loose coalitions on very broad regional lines: initially the hinterland as a whole against the Freetown area, subsequently the Northern Province and Western Area against the Southern and most of the Eastern Province. At a local level, where the main prize was local office, especially the Paramount Chieftaincy, the effect was to politicise factional divisions within chiefdoms, and hence to inhibit tribal or regional organisations; this was the case especially in the Mende areas. Where political competition was geared to gaining economic benefits, which had to be extracted from the centre rather than competed for in constant sum terms by local contestants, there were advantages in politicising regional, district or tribal identities: this happened most markedly in Kono, where district-wide demands for a more favourable share of the diamond revenues outweighed (except in the smallest and least affected chiefdoms) chiefdom factional conflict; similarly the APC gained northern support before 1967 from the belief that the north as a whole had been disadvantaged in its access to government services at the expense of the Mende areas.[11]

Though the electoral rules thus initially favoured those who controlled resources in the hinterland, whether these took the form of social status or communal identity, in the longer term these hinterland interests could not establish themselves, and the rules which benefited them withered away. The most obvious reason was the disunity expressed in both regional and local factional conflict; but this in turn was due to the hinterland's dependence on the centre for allocations of government funds and local offices. The result was that as the rules changed, those who held central resources – executive power, patronage, money, and ultimately force – were the gainers. The most striking example was the army takeover on the heels of the APC's electoral victory in 1967. This could not be sustained, and the APC's restoration after a further coup in 1968 resolved the direct confrontation between the holders of military resources on the one hand and electoral ones on the other. But Stevens' accession did not restore the government's responsiveness to hinterland electoral pressures so much as enable a new regime – though one with some popular backing – to gain access to the sources of control. Since by this time many tribal politicians had established themselves at the centre, in political parties, the army, and administrative posts, this shift back to the centre did not involve a commensurate shift in power to the Creoles. The adherence of many leading Creoles to Stevens' APC was however an important factor in enabling him to enact rule changes – a Republic with an executive President, a rigged election, the detention of opponents under emergency regulations – which had been vigorously opposed when attempted by Albert Margai a few years previously.

Would-be politicians in Sierra Leone have thus tended to operate by seeking sources of support from which to construct an independent political base, and have then sought to use this base to pursue political power at the centre, either in coalition with other politicians or, increasingly in recent years, by suppressing them. For hinterland politicians with regional connections, the most obvious place to look for such a base has been in local conflicts, either through the minutiae of factions at the chiefdom level or, for the more important operators, by seeking to mobilise the aspirations or discontents of tribal or regional groups; the succession of politicians who have sought to draw on the demands of the Kono diamond miners are a particularly clear example of this. Other politicians have looked to whatever material was closest to hand: in the case of army officers to the military, or in that of the Creole elite to the possibilities of advancement through the judiciary, the bureaucracy or the university, or through alliances with hinterland coalitions short of the skills which Creoles could provide. Some groups such as trade unionists and commoners in the chiefdoms have remained comparatively disadvantaged, despite the rise to power of the APC, with a broadly anti-chief ethos and an ex-trade unionist leader; but in general, everyone has been able to fight for his interests in the grand free-for-all of Sierra Leonean politics. Resources may change as the economy and society change, but there are no obvious and important ones simply waiting to be mobilised. The rules have tended to become the battling ground for conflicts between groups, reflecting at any time the current state of play between them.

This raises problems as to what the rules are and how they change which affect the analyst quite as much as the actor. Until 1967, the rule structure denoted a collection of formal and informal procedures and expectations which were beyond the direct control of any actor in the system, at first because they were imposed from outside by the colonial government, and subsequently because they were maintained by a rough balance of contending interests within the domestic arena. These rules changed in some respects, and attempts were made to subvert them, but it was nonetheless possible for them to be used to arbitrate in the 1967 election between the coalition of resources mustered by the APC and that mustered by the SLPP. Since then, and especially between 1967 and 1971, it has scarcely been meaningful to regard the rules as allocating power between different resources at all, since each change of power has been accompanied by a corresponding change in rules. In a sense, this is not a conceptual problem: it simply reflects the fact that politics in this period *has* been more uncertain, the constraints on actors have been more difficult for both them and others to codify than in earlier years. Looked at in another way, the breakdown of agreed rules means that the ultimate rule – that the winner is the actor who can muster the greatest force at the required place and time – comes into operation in their place. This indeed was the rule most in evidence in the crises of March 1967, April 1968, September 1970 and April 1971. The APC's ability to maintain itself in power since then may lead to more stable expectations, and the acceptance, however reluctant, of a set of rules to govern them.

In Liberia, by contrast, the rules have been held fairly constant, and the relationship between them and the resources in the hands of the central core has scarcely been at issue. What matters, rather, is the extent to which other resources and their holders can be admitted to a share in this structure, and conversely the extent to which excluded or undervalued resources remain outside as a potential danger to it. The core group's response to this problem, which its leaders have certainly recognised, has been to extend its own patronage networks into the hinterland, and to recruit the holders of those resources which are compatible with the existing structure. These are the resources derived from horizontal cleavage: wealth, status, education, and, most riskily, skills and rank in the armed forces. At the same time, by prohibiting the mobilisation of vertical cleavages below the national level, the core have sought to prevent hinterlanders from acquiring that combination of skills and local support which their Sierra Leonean equivalents used to bridge the gap between local and central legels of political activity. In Sierra Leone, the electoral rules greatly facilitated this process. In Liberia, it would be much more difficult to achieve, though it might be brought about through other rule changes, most obviously military intervention. The present rules are maintained on the assumption that so long as individuals from the hinterland can be associated with the core through the recognition of 'horizontal' resources such as education, wealth and status, they will not seriously need – and hence can be dissuaded from seeking – to mobilise 'vertical' resources derived from ethnic identity, with which to challenge the core itself. The principal means through which this co-operation has been achieved is the economic growth which so far has made political change in the hinterland a matter more of gaining access to constantly increasing jobs and opportunities, than of intensifying conflict for a given number of posts. The rapid increase through education of the numbers of people expecting such posts, and any sharp decline in the rate of economic expansion, are likely therefore to make it much harder to contain resources unmobilised within the present rules.

To summarise, many of the differences between the two countries can be characterised in the comparative coherence of the rules in Liberia, contrasted with the incoherence of those in Sierra Leone. In Liberia, economic resources, social status and political power all hang together within a single system which contains no appreciable internal contradictions. This stands or falls as a whole, and any actor involved in Liberian politics must either act within it or else rebel against it. Sierra Leone has no such single system of rules. It contains several alternative sets of rules, often irreconcilable with one another, which can be used by different actors and under different circumstances. The difficulty of reconciling the formal liberal democratic rules bequeathed by the colonial power with the authoritarian ones likewise inherent in the colonial tradition has already been noted. If therefore the army or the party in power calls on one set, while the opposition calls on another, there is no neutral rule structure in terms of which to arbitrate between the two. At the local level, the Paramount Chief must combine the rules and roles appropriate to a local community leader, an electoral politician and a government administrative agent. The rules of political allocation by party and patronage clash with those of legal and bureaucratic allocation by the judiciary and civil service. It is not necessary therefore either totally to act within the system or totally to reject it; it is necessary only to emphasise those elements in it, whether formal or informal, which favour one's own position. In this lies much of the confusion and surface instability which distinguish the Sierra Leonean polity from the Liberian.

CHAPTER 5

POLITICAL ALLOCATION AT THE CENTRE

THE STRUCTURE OF CENTRAL POLITICS

The rules and resources outlined in the last two chapters combine to form central political bargaining points which differ appreciably. One especially important consequence is that the centre itself has a rather different role and meaning within the overall political structures of the two countries. For both, it constitutes a collection of coercive and economic controls and institutions whose main features have already been outlined. In Liberia, it also serves as an autonomous focus for political identity and support – and also, potentially, for opposition. In Sierra Leone, where the central government can largely be equated with those politicians who are for the time being in power, this feature is conspicuously lacking. The results of this difference appear in all of the four aspects of central politics with which this essay is concerned; the ways in which politicians are recruited to office; the ways in which they combine and compete with one another within the central political arena; the opportunities and strategies for leadership which are open to them; and the role of force, either in support of the government or against it. These aspects of politics in turn affect the relationships between the institutions of central government noted in the last chapter.

POLITICAL RECRUITMENT

Political leaders in both countries have needed to be able to draw on some set of resources which distinguished them from the mass of the population, and in this sense enabled them to become members of an elite. They have needed, too, to make use of patronage and the opportunities which the political structures of the time provided. Nonetheless, the Liberian leaders may broadly be said to have made their way up as insiders, and the Sierra Leonean ones as outsiders, to the existing political establishment.

Liberia has had only two national leaders during the period covered by this study, both of them recruited essentially by central co-option. Neither Tubman nor Tolbert came from the very top families of the Americo-Liberian establishment, but each of them was born into an immigrant family which had some entrée to the elite. The Tubmans were well established in Maryland – which in itself placed them outside the main Monserrado families – so that W. V. S. Tubman was well placed to acquire a local base which enabled him to go to

Monrovia as one of the Maryland senators. He strengthened this base by hard work, by taking up local causes both as a Senator and through his private legal practice, and by the easy-going folksy manner expected of a Liberian politician. In Monrovia he built up central connections in the same manner, as well as through the Freemasonry and by marriage to a member of a leading Monserrado family. After a spell in the Supreme Court, he was selected as his successor by the outgoing President Barclay in 1943, and he was by then popular enough and well enough connected to make his election generally acceptable. President Tolbert was far more directly co-opted. His father, William R. Tolbert Sr, established the family fortunes, married into a prominent Cape Mount family, and gained the seat in the House of Representatives which his son took over in 1943. His elevation to the Vice-Presidency in 1951 was entirely at Tubman's bidding, and was generally ascribed to Tubman's desire to have a Vice-President too unpopular (and, especially, too tight-fisted) to become a rival. Nonetheless, Tolbert retained his base in the Vice-Presidency for nearly twenty years, married his daughter to the President's son, and saw his two brothers acquire influential positions in politics and commerce; by the time he took over as President in 1971, he had acquired a network of connections second only to Tubman's own.[1]

Of the Sierra Leonean leaders, Milton Margai was certainly in a favoured position, since he could combine his chiefly connections in Mendeland with his status as the first Protectorate doctor, to appeal to the two main elements in the hinterland elite; but he came to power by mobilising these elements against the Freetown establishment, and thus displacing the Creoles from leadership of the central government. Albert Margai had the same family advantages, and he gained the premiership eventually by manipulating the succession in Freetown after Milton's death in 1964. He was not, however, the automatic beneficiary even of the new hinterland establishment which Milton and the SLPP had brought to power; he had split away from the SLPP in 1958 and shown himself willing to mobilise outside resources even against his brother, and he came to power despite the hostility of many individuals in the party and administration. The most nearly co-opted of Sierra Leonean national leaders was Brigadier Lansana, whose two-day regime in 1967 rested on an unsuccessful attempt to combine his personal connections with Albert Margai with his control of the army; it failed because the combination was not accepted by the middle-ranking officers who by then were in a position to enforce a change of rules which favoured the army alone. The NRC regime thus represented a further infusion of outside leadership, even though most of its members came from one or other of the two strata – the Creoles and the hinterland chiefly families – whose members were best placed to seek elite positions. Stevens, finally, is in a sense the greatest outsider of them all, a man without a firm base in either ethnic identity, chiefly status, educational skills, or professional organisation. He was in opposition from 1958 until 1967, and succeeded in orchestrating a large enough coalition of excluded groups and politicians to defeat Albert Margai's government at the polls. After

Table 1. *Cabinet Ministers*

(*a*) *by Province/County of origin*

Sierra Leone	*Jan. 1963*	*May 1967*	*May 1973*
Western Area	5	2	6
Northern Province	4	2	12
Eastern Province	3	2	2
Southern Province	5	2	3
Total	17	8	23

Liberia	*Jan. 1964*	*Jan. 1968*	*May 1973*
Monserrado County	11	11	11
Other coastal Counties	5	5	6
Hinterland Counties	0	0	2
Total	16	16	19

(*b*) *by ethnic group*

Sierra Leone	*Jan. 1963*	*May 1967*	*May 1973*
Creole	5	2	6
Temne	4	2	7
Other Northern groups*	0	0	5
Mende	7	3	2
Other Southern groups†	1	1	2
Kono	0	0	1
Total	17	8	23

* Includes Limba, Yalunka, Koranko, Susu.
† Includes Sherbro, Krim, Gallinas/Vai, Kissi.

Liberia	*Jan. 1964*	*Jan. 1968*	*May 1973*
Americo-Liberian	12*	12†	11
Tribal: coastal Counties	4	4	6
Tribal: hinterland	0	0	2
Total	16	16	19

* Includes two Ministers of mixed Americo-Liberian/tribal descent.
† Includes one Minister of mixed Americo-Liberian/tribal descent.

(*c*) *by education*

Sierra Leone	*Jan. 1963*		*May 1973*
University: foreign	7		5
University: Sierra Leone	0		2
Secondary	8		10
Primary	0		4
Unknown	2		2
Total	17		23

Liberia	*Jan. 1964*	*Jan. 1968*	*May 1973*
University: foreign	9	9	13
University: Liberia	5	5	4
Secondary	1	1	0
Unknown	1	1	2
Total	16	16	19

Table 1 (*continued*)

(d) by age			
Sierra Leone	*Jan. 1963*		*May 1973*
Under 40	2		2
40–49	2		12
50–59	7		6
60 and over	4		1
Unknown	2		2
Total	17		23
Liberia	*Jan. 1964*	*Jan. 1968*	*May 1973*
Under 40	2	1	4
40–49	7	7	4
50–59	3	3	6
60 and over	3	4	3
Unknown	1	1	2
Total	16	16	19

Notes and sources

Sierra Leone names are taken from *Daily Mail*, Freetown, for January 1963 and May 1967, and from *Sierra Leone Gazette*, vol. 104 no. 38, 30 May 1973; figures for 1967 refer to members of the National Reformation Council; figures for 1973 include the President.

Liberia names are taken from *Liberia Official Gazette*, Monrovia, vol. 64 nos. 1/2 and 3/4, January–April 1964, and vol. 92 nos. 1/2, January–February 1968, and from *Liberian Government Directory 1973*; figures for all years include the President and Vice-President.

Details of place of origin, ethnic group, education, and age have been gained partly from publications and partly from personal informants. The publications include A & A Enterprises, *Directory and Who's Who* (Monrovia 1971), J. Dickie & A. Rake, *Who's Who in Africa*, *Daily Mail* (Freetown) 30 April 1968, Friedrich-Ebert-Stiftung, *African Biographies* (Bonn 1967 onwards), *Report of the Forster Commission* (Freetown 1968), and S. Taylor, *The New Africans*.

arrest and exile by the NRC, he ultimately reached the premiership in the wake of the privates' coup in 1968.

Similar mechanisms have shaped recruitment to middle-level leadership positions. A crude indication is provided by Tables 1–3, which give such information as I have been able to discover on the ethnic and regional origins of cabinet ministers, members of the legislature, and high central government officials between 1963 and 1973.[2] Despite their inadequacies, some useful patterns emerge. One of them, clearly, is that the Americo-Liberians control a much higher proportion of posts in Liberia than do the Creoles in Sierra Leone, except perhaps in the judiciary and the higher bureaucracy where the Creoles hold their own. However, the variations within countries and over time are equally instructive. Despite the Creoles' inability to control the top leadership positions, except under the peculiar circumstances of the Juxon-Smith regime, they have maintained a percentage of ministerial posts out of all proportion to their seats in the House of Representatives, which in turn exaggerate their numbers in the population as a whole. The differences between the Creole representation in the legislature and in the bureaucracy clearly reflect the different recruitment rules

Table 2. *Members of the Legislature*

(*a*) *By distribution of constituencies*

Sierra Leone	*1962*		*1967*		*1973*	
	O	PC	O	PC	O	PC
Western Area	12	0	12	0	12	0
Northern Province	18	5	20	5	32	5
Eastern Province	13	3	15	3	20	3
Southern Province	19	4	19	4	21	4
Total	62	12	66	12	85	12

(O = Ordinary Members; PC = Paramount Chief Members)

Liberia	*1962*		*1969*		*1973*	
	S	R	S	R	S	R
Monserrado	2		2	11	2	11
Other coastal Counties	8		8	19	8	24
Coastal Territories	0		0	5	0	5
Hinterland Counties	0		8	16	8	21
Total	10		18	51	18	61

(S = Senators; R = Representatives)

(*b*) *By party membership at election* (Sierra Leone ordinary members only)

Sierra Leone	*1962*			*1967*			*1973*		
	SLPP	APC	IND	SLPP	APC	IND	SLPP	APC	IND
Western Area	5	4	3	1	11	0	0	11	1
Northern Province	5	12	1	2	18	0	0	32	0
Eastern Province	5	4	4	11	2	2	0	20	0
Southern Province	13	0	6	14	1	4	0	21	0
Total	28	20	14	28	32	6	0	84	0

Notes and sources

Sierra Leone constituencies and results from Cartwright, *Politics in Sierra Leone*, Table 9:4 (for 1962); General Notice No. 394, reprinted in *Daily Mail* (Freetown), 26 April 1968 (for 1967); General Notice No. 369, *Sierra Leone Gazette*, vol. 104 no. 34, 16 May 1973 (for 1973).

Liberia constituencies from *Liberian Government Directory*, 1969 and 1973.

involved, and are much more marked than anything in Liberia where bureaucratic and legislative posts are both filled essentially by co-option. Even so, the Americo-Liberians are now in a minority in the House of Representatives and have barely half the seats in the Senate; the big difference here from Sierra Leone is that, both because of the True Whig Party monopoly and because of the separation of powers, this tribal majority cannot be converted into control of the executive.

In view of the Liberian central government's close association with a long-established urban elite, it is not surprising that ministers should on the whole be more highly educated there than in Sierra Leone, where many of them are recruited from the educationally backward hinterland. Age differences between

Table 3. *Senior Central Government Officials*

(*a*) *Permanent Secretaries and equivalents, by Province of origin*

Sierra Leone	*Jan. 1963*	*Jan. 1968*	*Sept. 1973*
Foreign	7	0	0
Western Area	7	6	16
Northern Province	0	3	1
Eastern Province	1	1	4
Southern Province	0	0	1
Total	15	10	22

This list includes all Permanent Secretaries, the Secretary to the Prime Minister or President, the Establishment Secretary, and the Secretary to the Cabinet, with their equivalents under the NRC regime.

(*b*) *Senior Assistant Secretaries and above, by Province of origin*

Sierra Leone	*Jan. 1963*	*Jan. 1968*	*Sept. 1973*
Foreign	9	2	0
Western Area	17	24	37
Northern Province	0	5	4
Eastern Province	1	2	9
Southern Province	1	4	8
Total	28	37	58

This list includes all Permanent Secretaries, Deputy Secretaries, Senior Assistant Secretaries, and other officials of equivalent rank.

Notes and sources

Names of officials from *Administrative Postings* lists, for 1 January 1963, 1 January 1968, and 1 September 1973; information on Province of origin obtained from personal informants.

Since no explicit distinction is made in Liberia between political and civil service appointments, no equivalent is available; the names of Under Secretaries, Assistant Secretaries and other subordinate executive officials are available in the same sources as for Table 1, but I was unable to obtain sufficiently comprehensive information on their areas of origin to be worth publishing.

the two countries are not so marked, but it is worth noting that the Liberian regime has not degenerated into a gerontocracy, but permits the recruitment of several ministers in their 30s, most but not all of whom belong to well-established families.

But these bare figures are inadequate, partly because (especially in Liberia) they make far too sharp a distinction between the tribal and immigrant communities, and partly because they show nothing of the mechanisms through which recruitment operates. For government ministers, formal recruitment is in each case by the President or Prime Minister, but the effective processes vary. In Liberia, the most important posts are held by men who have established themselves in the Americo-Liberian hierarchy, through ancestry, marriage, rank in community organisations such as the churches, the Freemasons and other fraternal organisations, as well as connections and experience in office. This is not to say that high officials get their positions because of their rank, say, in the Freemasons; it is rather that one's rank in the Craft and in the government are both indications of one's standing in the community as a whole. The President has considerable discretion in selecting individuals for particular positions, and over a period he may raise his protégés and diminish potential rivals, but – like a British party leader – he is surrounded by a small group of men who have a status approaching his own in the same community as himself.[3] Junior politicians, such as C. Cecil Dennis, Minister of Foreign Affairs, or Edwin Williams, Minister of Finance, make their way up within the same institutions, which thus help to impose common expectations and patterns of behaviour on their members. To some extent also, assimilated tribal men may ascend the same scale, though in recent years a few of these have been appointed to ministerial positions from outside the core community in order to bring in technical expertise and broaden the ethnic appearance of the government. A good example is the Minister of Information, Dr Edward Kesselly, a Loma man from Lofa County who takes no part in organisations such as the Masons. It is important to note, though, firstly that his political position is less stable as a result – having been projected into high office by the President, he could equally easily be abased; and secondly that he has no base in Lofa County, having gained his education and connections centrally, initially through his father's position as a general in the army.

In Sierra Leone there is no equivalent community, with its special institutions extending beyond the political sphere, through which recruitment can be organised. To some extent these exist among the Creoles, who equally use the Freemasons as a communal organisation, but this does not have the same relevance for the political system as a whole. In their place, ministerial recruitment has principally been based on position in the political party, or more broadly on a combination of prime ministerial or presidential favour and local influence. Since ministers have to be Members of Parliament, and until the early 1970s could always threaten to cross the floor to the opposition if their home region was neglected, they have often been recruited with an eye to representing all of the Provinces and at least most of the Districts in the Cabinet. The NRC formalised the same convention so as to avoid accusations of regional bias, by choosing two of its members from each of the three Provinces and the Western Area. In the Cabinet which followed the effective introduction of a single-party state in May 1973, however, the Northern Province and Western Area were heavily over-represented at the expense of the Southern and Eastern Provinces, indicating the President's increased freedom of action in selecting ministers.

Recruitment to subordinate executive positions in Liberia is not essentially different from the selection of ministers, though the lower one goes the slighter the appointee's connections are likely to be. Appointment to all executive posts is in principle – and to a large extent in practice – at the President's discretion, and has generally been used, most extensively by Tubman, as a source of patronage. There is no career scale up which civil servants work their way, but rather a procedure of appointing specific individuals to specific posts, in which they then stay for life or until they can once more bring their claims to the President's attention. A minister whose standing with the President is high enough, such as the late Stephen Tolbert, President Tolbert's brother and former Minister of Finance, may be able to make a clean sweep of existing officials and replace them with his own nominees. Some attempt is being made under the Tolbert administration to systematise lower level appointments through a Civil Service Bureau, and an Institute of Public Administration was set up in 1971.

Sierra Leonean civil service appointments are formally made by a Public Service Commission, except for those at Permanent Secretary level which are made by the President. By 1973, all five members of the PSC had been appointed since the APC came to power in 1968, and some of them were known for their party affiliation, giving some colouring to allegations that party patronage played an appreciable role in their appointment. The most notable thing about its composition in 1973, however, was that four of the five members were up-country men, replacing an earlier imbalance in favour of Creoles. The top civil service positions are inevitably politicised though appointments to them have to be made from those already well placed in the service; Albert Margai in particular appointed close personal followers, several of them Mendes, to key posts such as Establishment Secretary.

Overall, the, bureaucratic recruitment procedures in the two countries appear to be converging, as the possibilities for patronage in Sierra Leone become greater, and as the Liberians find the need to introduce public service procedures into parts at least of their inflated and heavily patronage-oriented administration.

PARTY AND FACTION

In neither country do political parties serve as the coherent and autonomous institutions of the Huntingtonian ideal, though they come rather closer to it in Liberia. In both, though, they reflect very clearly the general structure of the political system, so that their differences, and – such as they are – their similarities, are well worth investigation.

The True Whig Party of Liberia, founded in 1869 and continuously in power since 1877, is by far the oldest political party on the African continent and one of the oldest surviving parties in the world. Initially it was the party of the black Americo-Liberians against the original coloured elite,[4] but it has now for generations been associated with the governing community. As such, it is one of the institutions through which membership of the elite is maintained, and the place of individuals within it measured. The National Chairman of the party is one of the most powerful politicians in the establishment, and the current holder of the post, Postmaster-General McKinlay DeShield, has generally been reckoned under both Tubman and Tolbert as the second most important man in the country. It was he – so rumour has it – who more than anyone ensured a peaceful succession to President Tubman by refusing to accept any candidate but Vice-President Tolbert.

The TWP has been more open than other elite organisations to penetration by hinterlanders, especially in the nomination of members of the legislature, which is its single most important function. Despite its proliferation of offices – a feature common to any Liberian organisation – it scarcely exists as a continuous organisation. It is dormant except at nomination and election time, since it has no party policy nor ideology – except for its formal electoral platform – and takes no part either in supervising and controlling the government or in implementing policies itself. Its other main function is extractive: until 1972, the party deducted at source, by way of subscription, a twelfth of every government employee's salary, in two instalments of half a month's salary each. This money was never publicly accounted for, though presumably some of it went to build the party's impressive multi-storey headquarters in Monrovia. This levy, in itself a remarkable testimony to the system's extractive capacity, was abolished by President Tolbert as part of the liberalising programme by which he sought to establish himself after taking over the presidency.

While the single Liberian party is an expression of elite interests, the Sierra Leonean ones, equally characteristically, are largely umbrellas for factional coalitions. They have been maintained by the need to compete for and allocate office, and have expanded and contracted as calculations of advantage have led factional leaders to shift from one party to another. During the period of fairly open electoral competition, these shifts were continuous. Governing parties could always exert the centripetal pull of office, but as the coalitions they comprised grew beyond the optimum size, they were liable to desertions by disadvantaged politicians who fancied that their chances were better in opposition.[5] The amount of patronage available, and the number of factions competing for it, were such that even members of the governing coalition were likely to find themselves squeezed out of what they regarded as their fair share of the rewards. Some genuine convictions of policy and principle have been superimposed on this contest for office, but these have never been enough to create appreciable differences between parties which cannot be accounted for in factional terms.

The first of these factional splits was the breakaway by the Albert Margai and Siaka Stevens wing of the SLPP to form the PNP in 1958. This secession followed from Albert's narrow failure to capture the premiership and SLPP leadership from his brother Milton, and can be interpreted largely as an attempt to capitalise on the discontents among the 'outs' and the younger politicians with Milton's conservative leadership which this bid for the leadership revealed. As Cartwright well shows, the PNP's radicalism was symbolic rather than practical, and once the 1959 local elections had demonstrated the PNP's failure to mobilise the resources needed to oust the SLPP, Albert was very willing to try his hand once more within the governing party.[6] Stevens' refusal to return to the fold may partly be explained by the fact that, being out of Parliament at the time, he could not have gained office in the government. The first opposition group which he formed on his own, the Elections Before Independence Movement, was straight-forwardly a catch-all for anyone discontented with the SLPP coalition; its successor, the APC, was more specifically directed to the North and to sub-elites and wage-earners who had no place in the SLPP, but sought support wherever it could find it. Between 1961 and 1967, the SLPP consistently tried to bring over APC leaders through the resources implicit in power, while the APC played on SLPP ones by threatening the local support bases on which they still relied. The APC eventually proved the more successful, as the 1967 elections indicated, but in the process it acquired supporters – in the Creole establishment, for instance – who denied it any claim to be considered a radical party. This process was still more marked after 1968, when the APC's attempts to attract support previously denied it, among Mende chiefdom factions for example, turned it into just such a conglomerate as the SLPP had been before it, though one with a rather different balance of forces.

The most recent and for many purposes the most instructive example of Sierra Leonean party formation is the UDP's attempted breakaway in 1970. The ingredients – and several of the individuals – were the same as those involved in the formation of the APC. Once again some Temne politicians felt themselves to be squeezed out of the place in government which they regarded as their due, and, as during Albert Margai's premiership, members of the governing party felt threatened by the Prime Minister's attempts to establish his control. The government, inevitably, had failed to live up to the popular expectations created by its accession to power.[7] The secessionists – like the PNP leaders – reckoned that they could gain the support of the majority of the House of Representatives; or if that failed, they could win a general election in alliance with other opposition groups.[8] They were probably right. What they failed to reckon on was that they would be given no chance to muster their support either in Parliament or in the country. Before parliament met, the UDP leaders were – illegally but effectively – in jail, and the combination of office and coercion ensured that none of their potential supporters crossed over. Equally in the 1973 elections, the government detained opposition leaders under the State of Emergency regulations.

While the TWP has had only a rudimentary organisation because it is so closely associated with the governing group, Sierra Leonean parties have remained ill-organised for the contrary reason: any central party organisation could only be achieved by elevating one leader or faction in the party, and would therefore be resisted by the others. Milton Margai never attempted any organisational structure for the SLPP other than through the Paramount Chiefs or other patrons like the tribal headmen in Freetown; this helped MPs to establish local bases independent of the premier, but this was a constraint which Milton was prepared to work within. Albert was not, partly perhaps because he had – as he claimed – dynamic goals which required the party to serve as an agency for national unity instead of passively reflecting local factions, and partly because of the alluring example in Guinea and Ghana of single-party leaders unconstrained by the intra-party opposition which he had to put up with in Sierra Leone. He therefore tried to establish control over it through various devices, including membership drives, building up a central organisation, and attempting (sometimes successfully, sometimes not) to impose candidates of his choice on local constituency parties.[9] More even than his attempts to pulverise the opposition, this alienated support which he could ill afford to lose, since rebel SLPP members who refused to accept his leadership were a key group after the disputed 1967 election. Even after 1968, Albert Margai's legacy continued to divide the SLPP. Though he remained in exile in London, he refused to relinquish the leadership, and the party in Sierra Leone was split between the older generation of SLPP politicians led by M. S. Mustapha, and the younger members opposed to Sir Albert, led by Salia Jusu-Sherif. This further diminished the party's effectiveness under what would in any case have been the trying conditions of opposition.

The APC could not rely on chiefly connections to the same extent as the SLPP, and therefore had to organise itself more effectively; it exerted much more central control than the SLPP over matters like the selection of candidates. Even here, though, centralisation was impeded by analogous factors, specifically by an undercurrent of dissatisfaction with Stevens' leadership. A strong 'drop Stevens' faction emerged at the APC's 1966 Convention, but backed down in view of the approaching general election. Similarly in the manoeuvres over the proposed Republic between 1969 and 1971, several APC ministers were concerned to prevent Stevens from reaching the unassailable supremacy of an executive presidency; alternatively during the same period, a party organisation which was not under Stevens' direct control would probably have reflected and increased the strength within the party of the Temne leaders potentially opposed to him.

Since 1970 the role of auxiliary organisations has increased, though these organisations have scarcely been party-wide but have, rather, been managed by individual politicians enjoying the President's confidence. They include the APC Youth League, especially in Freetown, and the 'Peoples' Militia' formed in Samu Chiefdom, on the Guinea border in Kambia District. Their functions have been coercive rather than representative or policy-implementing, designed to provide a counter-weight to the army and to intimidate the opposition. Rival organisations have also been attached to factions within the APC, most obviously the two contestants for the women's section of the party in Freetown in 1972–3. The original organisation, informally linked with the party though not formally part of it, was the Congress of Sierra Leone Women led by Nancy Steele, a redoubtable Creole politician who for many years had been closely associated with Siaka Stevens. She made two enemies in S. I. Koroma the Prime Minister, whom she challenged for control of his Freetown constituency, and Mrs Rebecca Stevens, the President's wife; these formed a new organisation, the Women's Wing of the APC led by Mrs Stevens and Mrs Koroma. Members of the two factions, dressed in distinctive uniform skirts and blouses, clashed at several public functions, including the State Opening of Parliament in June 1972.[10] Mrs Steele was denied the party nomination in the 1973 elections but stood as an Independent for Freetown Central I; since her defeat the Congress has apparently become more or less defunct.

The clash was associated with other divisions within the party, notably that between S. I. Koroma and the Finance Minister and APC Secretary-General, C.A. Camara-Taylor, for the second place in the party and eventual succession to Stevens. Camara-Taylor, a Limba, had the longer record of service to the party and loyalty to its leader, but Koroma was promoted over his head due to the need to appoint a Temne to the Premiership in the aftermath of the UDP breakaway and the 1971 attempted coup. Koroma's ability to get his appointees selected in most of the contested nominations for the 1973 elections was thus significant, especially in view of the constitutional provision that the selection of a new President rests with the House of Representatives; in practice, this may not be so important as the control of coercive instruments, in which Koroma also appears to have the advantage. Factionalism thus continues within what is now effectively a single-party state, though equally the APC's office-holders have a lot that holds them together against any challenge from excluded groups. These factions appear to be rather more related to the divisions among the population at large, and rather less adequately controlled by institutions and social conventions, than those within the TWP.

Liberian factions, however, are none the less intense for being confined within a small governing community, and the ramifications of group-membership, office-holding and family connections through which they are pursued have been well described by Liebenow.[11] For the most part, they operate in an unpublicised way, best followed through government appointments, and the changes between the Tubman government of 1968 and the Tolbert one of 1973 are especially instructive. Several of the families connected with President Tubman's wife, including the Barclays and the Grimeses, had by 1973 disappeared – no doubt temporarily – from political view. So had Tubman protégés like Ernest Eastman, once the influential Under-Secretary of State, who became an ambassador; even Tubman's son, though married to Tolbert's daughter, was largely concerned with looking after his home base in Maryland. The Weeks family, prominent in politics and business under Tubman, were no longer represented in the higher reaches of government and were challenged in the commercial sphere by Stephen Tolbert's companies. In place of these, the Tolbert family itself was the most obvious gainer, with William in the Executive Mansion, his elder brother Frank as President pro tempore of the Senate, and his younger brother Stephen, until his death in 1975, as Minister of Finance and the country's leading entrepreneur. Their associates in the Dennis clan were also in the ascendant with two of its younger members in charge of Foreign Affairs and Commerce. As against this, a few established politicians held their positions all through.

LEADERSHIP

The role of leaders in any political system indicates in a very sensitive way the constraints which the prevailing rules place on political activity, and the opportunities which they allow politicians to pursue their goals. This is most obvious for national leaders, but it is equally true of middle level actors who, lacking the comparative freedom of action of a President or Prime Minister, must calculate even more carefully the strategies designed to secure the best use for their limited resources.

In a strategic sense, leadership roles in both countries have been basically passive. Neither country has had any government which could be called radical, let alone revolutionary, or which had any very clearly articulated goals for effecting social change. For top-level leaders, no goal in either country has matched in importance the basic one of maintaining their own position. The reasons for this passivity, which differs markedly from the goals of their common neighbour, Guinea, can however be ascribed to different features of the two countries' governments. Sierra Leonean regimes have never been able to generate sufficient united fervour to support a nationalist party based on a common programme for change; the division between the Creoles and the hinterland, which cut off several would-be radical leaders among the Freetown intelligentsia from their potential supporters, is symptomatic of this, and is summed up in the career of I. T. A. Wallace-Johnson. Wallace-Johnson was for over two decades – from the 1930s into the 1960s – one of the most radical anti-colonialists on the west coast of Africa; but unlike Nkrumah, who found the material for his Convention People's Party (CPP) readily at hand, he was unable to find or to create any effective organisation through which to muster support, even during the post-war period when other nationalist leaders were doing so elsewhere in West Africa. Nor did any younger leader take his place, as might have been expected had sufficient support been available. The Liberian government, for its part, is so much the instrument of an elite that it is automatically inhibited from pursuing any policy likely to endanger that elite's position.

These maintenance goals lend themselves to a transactional style of leadership, and the two grand old men of their countries' recent history, Milton Margai in Sierra Leone and W. V. S. Tubman in Liberia, were both masters of this technique. The most important resource at the leader's disposition in each case was office, which could readily be bargained for political support. For Sir Milton, this was largely a matter of maintaining some balance among members of his own party, while seducing opposition leaders to join it. The perfect example is the crossover of three of the four Kono MPs from the SLPIM to the SLPP in July 1963. Before it, Kono had been starved of development funds and was unrepresented in the Cabinet; afterwards, the central government grants flowed into Kono, and one of its MPs became a Cabinet Minister.[12] Tubman was in a much stronger position, since his political base was more secure and subordinate politicians scarcely had the option of opposition open to them, but the essence of the transaction was the same: support and information exchanged for office and money. Tubman, too, was able to strengthen his hold by offering his appointees opportunities for corruption which they could scarcely decline, but which could be held against them should any excuse be needed for their dismissal.

But although a transactional style is conservative in the sense that it subordinates purposive government action to the need to maintain a balance among existing political groups, it nonetheless lends itself fairly well to one of the most important roles of leadership, that of associating new groups and resources with the existing political order. While the dynamic leader characteristically needs to divest himself of sources of support which constrict the plans which he wants to carry out, the transactional one can bring a broad range of often conflicting interests into the bargaining process which he orchestrates. Thus Milton Margai and W. V. S. Tubman, in one sense the most conservative of modern Sierra Leonean and Liberian leaders, were in another sense highly innovatory. Both of them extended the range of bargaining structures to include both coastal and hinterland elements, even though their different origins and the rules within which they operated affected the ways in which and extent to which this was done. Milton's achievement was first to organise the hinterland elites to take part in central government, and subsequently to extend the process so as to bring the Creoles back into a reasonably amicable system of exchanges under the SLPP; he was much less successful with sub-elite pressures, which had to await incorporation through the Kono political parties and the APC. Tubman, chosen (like all Liberian Presidents) through co-option from within the coastal elite, then brought at least some hinterland groups into politics in a way which both extended political participation and increased his own freedom of action by freeing him from over-reliance on his initial supporters, and enabling him to manage the transactions between coast and hinterland. The unsuccessful attempt by Tubman's former patron, ex-president Edwin Barclay, to oust his chosen successor in the 1955 presidential election, shows this process very well.

The two nearest approaches to a more dynamic leadership style have been Sierra Leone's two briefest regimes (excluding Lansana's two days), those of Albert Margai and the NRC. These both attempted, though in different ways, to impose a central leadership on the country and to suppress political factions or subordinate them to it. Both attempts failed, because the bases on which both Albert and the NRC tried to establish themselves crumbled under the weight which this strategy placed on them. Albert's base was the SLPP, which he tried to convert from an amalgam of local leaders into a disciplined personal following. This was completely at variance with his brother's technique of accepting factions and working through them, and since he inherited the party which his brother had created, it is scarcely surprising that it proved inadequate for his purpose. The methods which he used, and the failure revealed by the 1967 election, have already been described.

Whereas Albert Margai was constantly constrained by the need to work through the SLPP and the parliamentary system, the NRC suspended the constitution, dissolved the political parties, and used the army as a power base. It did not ally itself with any group of politicians, partly at least because there was scarcely any group available for the purpose: having ousted Lansana because it saw him as the agent of the defeated SLPP it could not look there; and the APC, having won the election and seen its leader sworn in as Prime Minister, had then been deprived of power by the NRC itself. The NRC is generally credited with some useful restorative measures, especially in dealing with the economy. It also put a damper on factional conflict by removing temporarily most of the procedures and institutions through which it was expressed, even though some of its own members were involved in local political disputes. Majors Jumu and Kai-Samba in particular were closely related to participants in the intricate affairs of Nongowa Chiefdom at Kenema. Despite the histrionic claims of its Chairman, Brigadier Andrew Juxon-Smith, the NRC was never able to do more than paper over the tribal divisions which it had set itself to dissolve, and it never began to create any institutional structure other than the army through which this could be done. It was therefore highly vulnerable to strains in the army itself, and collapsed when these were politicised through a mixture of lower rank discontent and northern ethnic sympathy for the APC.

For a final comparison of top leadership styles, it is useful to look at the strategies adopted by Siaka Stevens and William Tolbert when they took over in Sierra Leone and Liberia in 1968 and 1971 respectively. In each case, they faced an immediate need to establish themselves in office: for Tolbert because of the hiatus created by the death of a dominant leader, and for Stevens because of his uncomfortable ride to power on the backs of a group of mutinous soldiers. In each case, then, they had to appropriate for their own support the most suitable resources available. For both of them the immediate reaction was to set up a government based on compromise and continuity, which helped to tide over the short-term problem of succession while keeping their options open for later. In Tolbert's case this meant keeping Tubman's cabinet; in Stevens' it meant constructing a coalition drawn from APC, SLPP and independent Representatives. In addition, they both sought pledges of support from every available source of organised opinion. Stevens spent the first month after his appointment in receiving congratulations from an astonishing variety of organisations, ranging from the Sierra Leone Labour Congress and the market women to the Moslem Association and the representatives of the Countess of Huntington's Connexion.[13] Tolbert went to the main army camp in Monrovia on the day after he was sworn in as President, to receive the allegiance of the armed forces, and thereafter a steady stream of loyal delegations made their way to the Executive Mansion.[14] Both leaders also sought to use their recognition abroad in order to strengthen their appeal for legitimacy at home, though Tolbert with his steadier home base was much freer to indulge in diplomatic trips, while Stevens was confined to Freetown.

From then on, the patterns diverge. For Stevens, leadership skills largely consisted in refining the bases of his factional coalition, seeking to free himself bit by bit from dependence on potentially hostile groups. The SLPP members of the coalition cabinet were squeezed out of office by election petitions which resulted in their 1967 election victories being annulled; in the resulting by-elections the APC found itself supporters in the SLPP strongholds in Mendeland by taking up the cause of chiefdom factions opposed to the sitting members, thus – with the help of government pressure – undercutting them on their home ground. Within the APC, he conducted a long process of bargaining over the introduction of a republican constitution, waiting for his opponents to declare themselves by splitting off to form the UDP before striking back decisively with the State of Emergency. In the highly divided army, likewise, an attempt to oust him by one faction was countered by the support of others. In this way, he took the gradual steps to consolidate his power which culminated in his elevation to the executive Presidency in April 1971. Thus he pursued the aims of Albert Margai by the methods of Sir Milton, putting forward no programmes and taking no initiatives except in response to the needs of factional bargaining and personal control. The policy vacuum in the Sierra Leone government may partly be due to Stevens' personal lack of policy goals, but is equally the result of a leadership style geared to factional manipulation.

In Liberia, the constraints on Tolbert were fewer as well as being different. His need was to demonstrate the capacity for active leadership which is expected of a President in such a way as to make himself popular, establishing a personal style without upsetting the fundamental features of Tubman's regime. He did this very skilfully by ending a number of specific abuses associated with the Tubman period, a move which enabled him to present himself as a dynamic and liberalising leader. One obvious target was Tubman's network of paid informers; Tolbert dismissed two top security officers and ordered them to repay embezzled funds, announcing that the money released from payment to informers was to be used for a pension scheme. He gained support from all government employees by abolishing the compulsory subscription of one month's salary to the True Whig Party, and permitted greater freedom for the press. The personality cult so marked under Tubman was to some extent played down, by shifting the annual national celebration from the President's birthday to independence day, and by proposing a limitation on the number of terms for which a President could hold office. His appointments strengthened his appeal to the hinterland and to the younger educated technocrats in the government. A stream of well publicised slogans flowed from the Executive Mansion. Certainly some of the new presidential dynamism was counter-productive. Tolbert's practice of making surprise visits to government offices to ensure that officials were at work resulted in the almost accidental and generally regretted dismissal of the Minister of Education, G. Flamma Sherman, who was not there on time. More seriously, one of Tolbert's pet schemes, the National Fund-Raising Rally, gave rise to just the same kinds of exaction as had, it seemed, been ended with the abolition of the TWP subscription. The prominence of the Tolbert family, with the President's elder brother Frank as President of the Senate and younger brother Stephen as Minister of Finance, reinforced these suspicions, and his hard-line attitude to rural tax-collection also put pressure on officials in the Counties. But even these cases are examples of a capacity for executive initiative, made possible by the President's comparatively secure position, which the Sierra Leonean system seems to lack.

The converse of the Liberian President's greater powers of initiative is the comparatively lower degree of initiative available in Liberia to middle-level leaders. The opportunities available to would-be politicians to operate outside the True Whig Party and the presidential patronage system are extremely restricted, even if they care to bank on the risky gamble of the entire Liberian system of government being overthrown. In Sierra Leone, they have frequently had the chance to opt for opposition; and even in those periods such as the NRC regime or the APC government after 1973 when the opportunities for formal opposition have been restricted, it has been possible for politicians to withdraw temporarily from the scene, either at home or in exile, in the hope that another turn of the wheel would bring them back again. For Liberian politicians the TWP regime, like it or not, appears to be a fixture; no Sierra Leonean government can present a similar appearance of stability.

In the short-term, too, Liberian ministers are more directly dependent on the President than their Sierra Leonean counterparts. They are appointable at will, without qualifications such as the Sierra Leone requirement that they be members of the House of Representatives. Some of them are protected by their family connections, though by no means all of them have these and only the Vice-President and the half-dozen or so most influential ministers are immune from instant dismissal. Several of Tolbert's ministers have been summarily ejected, including Flamma Sherman at Education as already noted, and Henry Andrews at Information for making a single unwise remark which threatened the foreign community. Once dismissed, moreover, there is no standby such as a seat on the parliamentary backbenches. Former ministers have to go into private employment, through their own profession or business or perhaps with a foreign corporation, while they try to make their way gradually back into favour; if they are particularly unwise or unlucky, they may find themselves in jail accused of subversion or embezzlement. This helps to explain the deference shown to the President, and the enormous amount of time which ministers and other politicians spend waiting on him, not only for business reasons but for minor ceremonial occasions like awaiting his return at Monrovia airfield from a day trip to a neighbouring country.

There is something of the same ritual deference in Sierra Leone, but the ministers have rather more to bargain with. For one thing, the President or Prime Minister has to draw his ministers from the restricted field of the House of Representatives. Before 1973, this consisted of fewer than eighty members, of whom twelve were Paramount Chiefs who could scarcely hold department portfolios, and a variable minority of the rest were in opposition. A very high proportion of government MPs therefore held office as ministers or deputy ministers; in the first Republican Cabinet of May 1971, for example, it came to twenty-eight out of the forty-eight APC Representatives. Despite this lack of choice, the Prime Minister or President has constantly been under pressure to increase the number of departments so as to provide more ministerial positions, and hence satisfy more factions and individuals. Sir Milton Margai, who defended the size of his Cabinet on the grounds that it broadened representation,[15] had fourteen departmental ministers in January 1963, with three regional ministers and two Paramount Chiefs as ministers without portfolio. Ten years later, the number of departmental ministers had grown to twenty. Thus ministers are aware that they represent particular interests or districts which the leader cannot afford entirely to ignore. On the other hand, though, the attractions of office are too great for all but a very few politicians voluntarily to turn them down when the chance of a portfolio comes their way.

The more fluid situation in which Sierra Leonean politicians operate increases uncertainty, and makes it harder to keep expectations in line with reality. In Liberia, the limitations on what one can achieve are clearer, and the requirements in support and apprenticeship for reaching a post such as Vice-President or Senator are readily understood. In Sierra Leone, expectations are less stable, and politicians may come to regard themselves as being entitled to positions for which their support is actually quite inadequate. Some such miscalculation underlay the attempt by Stevens' disenchanted former supporter, Brigadier John Bangura, to seize power with a tiny body of troops in 1971. On the civilian side, the clearest example is that of Dr Mohamed Forna. A medical doctor, he first entered politics rather late in the day as APC candidate for a Tonkolili constituency in the 1967 election. He spent some of the NRC period in exile with Stevens in Guinea, and after the 1968 return to civilian rule he was rapidly promoted to be Minister of Finance. He proved extremely able, and frequently acted as Prime Minister while Stevens was abroad. He thus acquired expectations of the premiership, the disappointment of which was evidently one factor in his secession from the APC to the UDP in 1970. For a Liberian politician of similar standing, the ambition would have been manifestly unreasonable, and the means taken to achieve it impossible.

VIOLENCE AND COERCION[16]

It is scarcely possible, nor would it be very helpful, to say whether Liberia is more coercive than Sierra Leone or vice-versa. It is a question, rather, of the forms which coercion takes in the two systems, and of the degree and type of violence which each of them contains and, possibly, provokes. Levels of coercion are unmeasurable because the forms which it takes are so different that no adequate common indices could be devised to compare them. In Liberia, it tends to be tacit, muted, and pervasive, in the sense that strong constraints exist against many kinds of political action taking place at all. Coercion is therefore a matter of policing the overall structure of political allocation; and since this structure has scarcely (yet, at any rate) been systematically or seriously challenged this has largely meant maintaining the boundary between permissible and impermissible political activity, and disciplining those who stray beyond it. In Sierra Leone, by contrast, the boundary between permissible and impermissible activity is a hazy and disputed one. The formal rules stipulating a peaceful and democratic liberty to express opinions and form political organisations have been widely transgressed both by government, in suppressing activities legitimate under these rules, and by non-governmental groups in resorting to violence outside them. Coercion in Sierra Leone has thus been much more open and specific, and it has been necessary not only for policing the boundaries of permissible political activity, but for maintaining several of the regimes themselves in power. Violence has been used, sometimes successfully, in order to overthrow regimes, and the uncertainty of rules is such that an area exists in which violence may be used as an instrument of policy.

Specific cases of violence and coercion in Liberia are comparatively few. The only adequately proved attempt to use violence to displace the government since Tubman's accession has been an attempt to assassinate him in 1955, which followed the election campaign of that year in which ex-President Edwin Barclay stood against Tubman; this is the one recent case in which political conflict within the immigrant community has, so to speak, escaped from the rules in which the community has encased it.[17] There have been several other reported plots, but none of them has got very far, and some of them may well have been invented or exaggerated by the government in order to discipline particular politicians whom the President presumably wished to cut down to size; they fit well into the pattern of policing boundaries. In February 1963, a Grebo Colonel, D. T. Thompson, was arrested on a charge of plotting to assassinate the President; he is reported to have said that 'if 250 Togolese soldiers could kill President Olympio and overthrow his Government, an army of 5,000 in Liberia can do wonders'.[18] In October 1970 General George T. Washington, a former Chief of Staff and a Kru, was alleged to have planned the assassination of the Secretary of Defense.[19] Both these cases indicated Tubman's manipulation of rivalries within the armed forces, especially among hinterland officers. Two other sedition trials in 1963 implicated relatives of leading politicians.[20] Since Tolbert's accession, there has been one analogous case in the trial of Prince Browne, an Assistant Minister of Defense who with two tribal lieutenant colonels was found guilty of conspiring to kill the President and his brother in the VIP lounge of the international airport outside Monrovia.[21] All of these charges have been vigorously denied by the alleged plotters, and it is hard to know how seriously to take them.

One feature of the trials both of Prince Browne and of Henry Farnbulleh, the Vai whose attempts to mobilise hinterland opinion led to his imprisonment in 1968, was the vociferous support given to the defendants by Liberian students in the courtroom. The University of Liberia has become the main source of overt opposition to the government, with several student publications going so far as they dare in criticism of it, and several other educational establishments were closed as a result of student unrest in 1974.[22] The government has been in two minds over how to deal with them and with other potential opponents such as Liberia's veteran pamphleteer Mr Albert Porte; the liberalisation of the press, which Tolbert introduced as a popular measure shortly after his accession, may thus become counter-productive. Henry Farnbulleh was released and given a post on Tolbert's staff, but had not been there long when he disagreed with the President and was dismissed. The strains involved in combining the existing government structure with the extension of educational resources are thus gradually becoming greater.

Though the rules in Liberia are restrictive, they nevertheless only sporadically need to be publicly enforced. It is otherwise in Sierra Leone, where the difficulties of maintaining a government in power make coercive methods attractive and often essential. The method most often resorted to is the simple detention of opposition politicians. Stevens himself and several other APC leaders celebrated independence day in 1961 in jail, under a state of emergency prompted by the belief that the APC planned to disrupt the occasion with acts of sabotage.[23] Albert Margai, for all his vaunted desire to smash the opposition and his proposals for a single-party state, did not however simply lock up his opponents. The SLPP brought several libel actions against APC newspapers though it did not ban them, and it harassed opposition supporters in the chiefdoms; but its bark was much worse than its bite. It did not, for instance, try to bring in a Preventive Detention Act.[24] Coercion since the military intervention in 1967 has been much more marked, as a result partly of the introduction of military resources which are implicitly committed to the use of force – whether to sustain a government or oppose it – and partly of the government's reduced willingness to tolerate opposition. Though the government announced the discovery of a military plot against it in February 1967,[25] the following month's takeover was the first ever use of violence to try to displace a government. Further cases followed: the NRC's ousting of Lansana, the Anti-Corruption Revolutionary Movement's (ACRM's) ousting of the NRC in April 1968, and the attempted coup in March 1971. In July 1974 a bomb exploded at the home of the Finance Minister, C. A. Camara-Taylor, and a large number of opposition politicians and ex-soldiers were immediately detained.[26]

Violence in turn has led to coercion. The NRC has been the most explicitly coercive, since – taking power from a newly installed and popularly elected government – it could not generate the popular support which greeted, say, the Ghanaian NLC in 1966. Several people were killed in rioting in Freetown after the takeover, and leading politicians were detained, though these were later allowed either to leave the country or to retire to private life. The Stevens government after 1968 made the most systematic use of detentions, aided by the state of emergency which was in force in 1968–9 and continuously for five years after 1970. Whenever crises arose – during the 1968 by-elections in the South, the UDP affair in 1970, or the general election in 1973 – it rounded up opponents for temporary detention, releasing them once the trouble died down. The opposition press, too, suffered periodic crackdowns, and only the efforts of a few indomitable and oft-detained journalists kept it in sporadic existence.[27] On occasions such as nomination day for the 1973 elections, the government showed itself prepared to exercise whatever coercion was necessary to stay in power, and to suppress the opposition violence which resulted, with some loss of life especially in Freetown. Opposition leaders however were generally not jailed for long periods – unlike their experience in Nkrumah's Ghana – and not until 1971 did the government go to the extreme step of executing an opponent. This was Brigadier John Bangura, who was involved in the abortive, and ludicrously mismanaged, coup in March 1971, and who ironically had been Stevens' main supporter in the army in 1967–70.[28] The officers involved in the NRC, though tried for treason, were released in 1973. Ex-Brigadier Lansana was rearrested after the bomb attack the following year, and was executed in July 1975, together with seven other people including two of the former APC ministers who had defected to the UDP, Mohamed Forna and Ibrahim Bash-Taqi.[29] As so often in such cases, it is not clear whether the charges were framed. What *is* clear is the continued role of violence and coercion in Sierra Leonean central politics.

There is equally a difference between the two countries in the historical development of the instruments of coercion and their consequent relations with the holders of political power. In Liberia, since the foundation of the first settlements, force has frequently been needed first to defend and subsequently to extend the area under the government's control. The armed forces have thus been closely associated with the governing community, particularly through the militia in which all able-bodied citizens used to be expected to serve; many leading politicians, including President Tubman, thus had some military experience. This association has declined, as the militia has lapsed into a formality, and its place has largely been taken by a regular army. This force, the Liberian National Guard, is actually appreciably larger than its Sierra Leonean equivalent, with a strength of about five battalions and detachments in each County. It has a far higher proportion of hinterlanders at all levels than any other national institution; in November 1973, two of the three generals on the active list were Lomas from Lofa County and about half the other senior officers on the headquarters staff were also tribal men; the proportion of hinterlanders among the rank and file is presumably very much higher. This fact has not been lost on hinterlanders anxious for a redistribution of central political power: pamphlets issued in 1968 and 1969 by a clandestine group called the Aborigines' Liberation Front were especially directed at the army, and one of them ended with the startling slogan: 'LONG LIVE AFRICAN SOCIALISM! LONG LIVE LIBERIAN MILITARISM!'.[30] The government has been equally aware of it, as the various plots and conspiracies already noted indicate, and any eventual radicalisation of the Liberal political system must inevitably involve the military. Until the time of writing, however, it has been kept out of direct involvement in the political arena. Other instruments of control include the police, the courts – in which the elite, with its pursuit of legal skills, is well established – and the complex networks of informers with which Tubman, especially, surrounded himself.

In Sierra Leone, the local battalion of the Royal West African Frontier Force was until 1961 under the direct control of the colonial government. After independence it had to adjust itself, like other local actors, to a situation in which its original point of reference had been removed. One such means of adjustment was the appointment of a Force Commander, David Lansana, who had close family ties with the SLPP leadership; but this scarcely served the purpose since the resulting subordination of the military after the 1967 elections to the political requirements of Albert Margai was not accepted by its middle-ranking officers. Thus the factionalism of Sierra Leonean politics first sucked the army into the political arena and then fragmented it. The NRC regime ended with the arrest and detention of almost the entire officer corps by their privates and NCOs. For several months after the return to civilian rule in 1968, these officers were imprisoned by their own soldiers in conditions worse than those for ordinary convicts.[31] They were gradually released and reinstated from November 1968 onwards, but the tensions between them and their former jailers, some of whom had by then been commissioned, were acute. Hence when the army next tried to intervene in politics, in March 1971, only a fraction of it did so and that in a highly disorganised way.

In this crisis, Stevens called on military help from Guinea in order to control his own chaotic army. In this as in so many respects, he was putting into effect measures first threatened by Albert Margai. There was indeed a common logic in this, in that in each case the control of factional conflict seemed to require a force which would not be fragmented in its turn, and hence a return to external sources of coercion. Other African states in similar circumstances have sometimes turned for help to the former metropole or other extra-continental powers.[32] In Sierra Leone, British help would scarcely have been acceptable, even had Britain been willing to supply it, and Sekou Touré's Guinea provided a neighbour which – unlike Liberia – was only too willing to fish in the troubled waters of an adjacent state. Albert's 1967 defence agreement with Guinea was never activated. The 1971 pact originated after the 1970 invasion of Guinea and was negotiated during February 1971, at a time when members of Sekou Touré's PDG were already exciting comment by appearing on the platform at APC rallies;

Liberia was also invited to join, and politely agreed in principle but did nothing further about it. Immediately after the March 1971 affair, Stevens flew to Conakry to conclude the agreement, under which several hundred Guinean troops came to Freetown to guard Stevens himself and vital installations. They were gradually reduced in number and the last ones left in March 1973.

In their place, other coercive organisations have been developed by the government to check or supplement the ordinary army and police. Some of these derive from the APC youth groups who were trained in guerilla warfare in Guinea during the NRC regime. The counter-coup of April 1968 took place before they could be used, but they remained in being and returned to Sierra Leone, where they appear to have formed the nucleus of a paramilitary force being trained by Cuban (and according to some reports Algerian or Chinese) instructors at camps in Samu Chiefdom, Kambia, and Jui in the Western Area.[33] They appear to be separate from the armed Internal Security Unit of the police, which was much in evidence during nominations for the 1973 elections, and from the vigilante squads of individual APC politicians. Finally, there are the ordinary Sierra Leone Police Force, and the Chiefdom Police whose integration into the national force has been announced but had not yet been implemented by April 1973. Thus, in Sierra Leone the sources of coercion appear to be coming to correspond more closely with the distribution of central political power, whereas in Liberia they are moving away from identification with the central elite. It is still too soon to say whether patterns of coercion are becoming more stable in Sierra Leone, but not too soon to indicate that they may be becoming less stable in Liberia.

RULES, CHANGE AND CENTRAL ALLOCATION

In summary, differences in rules appear to account quite satisfactorily for the variations in central political allocations between the two countries, at any rate – in Sierra Leone, at least – up to 1967. In each country, a set of rules was established which provided for recruitment to the most important political roles, and in turn help to explain the prevalent forms of political organisation, the opportunities and constraints available to leaders, and the uses of violence or coercion. In each case, too, these rules were beyond the immediate control of those who might reckon themselves to be disadvantaged by them. In Sierra Leone, the electoral system was initially imposed by the colonial government over the vociferous opposition of Creoles who saw themselves as the natural heirs to the colonial regime; however, Creoles were given some stake in the system, and by the time of Albert Margai's premiership they had come to look to it for the defence of their own interests. In Liberia, the hinterland had little say in instituting the system of co-option through the True Whig Party, but here too the main potential opponents of the rule structure – the educated elements in the hinterland were given some opportunity for participation through it.

Both countries were thus provided, initially at least, with reasonably effective systems for central allocation. In Sierra Leone, the loose coalitional parties provided opportunities for local representation which did not lead to irreconcilable central conflicts. The superimposition of varying lines of cleavage – immigrant/indigene, tribal, factional – prevented any single division from assuming overriding importance, and the channelling of participation through a fairly self-confident hinterland chiefly and educated elite helped to keep party competition within manageable bounds. Liberian participation was much more closely channelled through the immigrant core, but this core was flexible enough to allow both for factional conflict within its own ranks and for some incorporation of outsiders.

The Sierra Leonean system was the more immediately precarious, since this depended not on any single group with a strong vested interest in maintaining the existing structure, but rather on a balance between competing groups each of which hoped to achieve some of its objects through it. It is possible to see the 1967 elections as a vindication of the effectiveness of representative democracy, which allowed the people to replace an unwanted set of leaders, and was only sabotaged by the intervention of a few strategically placed individuals.[34] However, the fact that constraints on these individuals were not enough to prevent them calling in the army to prevent a transfer of power, and the further subversion of the representative system by both the NRC and the Stevens government, call for a fuller explanation. One element in this must be the uneasy juxtaposition, in the representative system, of the local resources on which the government relied for its election, and the central coercive and distributive ones on which it relied for its maintenance in power. Another is the lack of a normative commitment to the electoral rules by those who expected to gain by breaking them. This is clear enough in the case of Albert Margai and his SLPP supporters who between 1964 and 1967 sought to impose a centralised single-party state and to dismantle the constraints provided by the judiciary, the constitution, and the electoral system. It is no less clear, however, in the case of those who successfully opposed these very moves. Cartwright has clearly shown that the APC's opposition to the single-party state in 1965–6 was based not on any objections in principle, but merely on the fact that it would be Albert Margai and the SLPP who ran it,[35] and his judgement is confirmed by the APC's own suppression of the opposition once it came to power. Equally, while Sir Albert's proposals were bitterly opposed by the Creole professional community which had long regarded him with enmity,[36] there was little such opposition to similar measures by the APC, in which Creoles were well represented. The formal rules thus suffered from a lack of support both from normative rules and, eventually, from pragmatic ones as well. The rules imposed in their place since 1971 do not raise the same conflict between central and local resources, and the failure of various attempts to overset them may provide them with pragmatic acceptance, but there is no indication that they have achieved any normative support.

The Liberian system of central allocation is more consistent, and has greater vested interests in its maintenance. As a result, it has been able to distribute offices and rewards in a way which has only recently started to be publicly challenged, and which has needed only a small amount of overt coercion. However, the Liberian rules are no less dependent than the Sierra Leonean ones on the need to accommodate the interests of those who control important resources. This has become increasingly obvious with the extension of the resources, especially educational and coercive ones, in the hands of groups outside the original immigrant core. Hence, while in the short run rules may provide a fairly satisfying explanation of differences in political allocations, in the longer run their capacity to order resources is limited.

CHAPTER 6

CENTRE AND PERIPHERY

THE STRUCTURE OF LOCAL POLITICS

Local politics is important not only at the local level. Certainly, the politics of those areas of their countries in which most Liberians and Sierra Leoneans live are worth considering in their own right; but, more than that, the relations between the central government and its peripheral counterparts or extensions form an integral part of the political system as a whole. Local arenas offer resources which are relevant to the central one, just as local actors in turn need to adapt to the opportunities and exactions which the centre places upon them. This chapter examines the terms on which the resulting exchanges between local and central resources take place, the effects which these exchanges have on political life at the local level, and the instruments through which they are conducted. It aims to show both the similarities in these respects between Sierra Leone and Liberia, and the differences which arise from the general features of the two systems which have already been noted.

The formal hierarchy of local government in each country links the base unit of local administration with the central government in the coastal capital. The levels in this hierarchy, and the main officials at each, are outlined in Figure 1. For most purposes, the chain of command runs from the central government to the County or District to the Paramount Chiefdom, though in Sierra Leone some allocations, especially of central government services, are made at the Provincial level. The Liberian District is an intermediary between County and chiefdom for which no equivalent exists in Sierra Leone, and is of only minor importance. One further difference is that Senators and Representatives are selected at the County level in Liberia, whereas in Sierra Leone Representatives are selected for single-member constituencies, with an additional Paramount Chief Representative for each District.

This hierarchy itself reflects some common features of the two administrations, emphasising the role of the centre as a source of extraction, allocation, and ultimately coercion. The sovereignty of the centre, and the ability of whoever holds power there to impose and if need be enforce its initiatives on peripheral actors is a fact well recognised at the local levels of both systems. The centre's economic role astride the trade in exported primary produce and imported goods is also a constant, to be considered in the next chapter. Nonetheless, the previously examined differences between the two systems account for

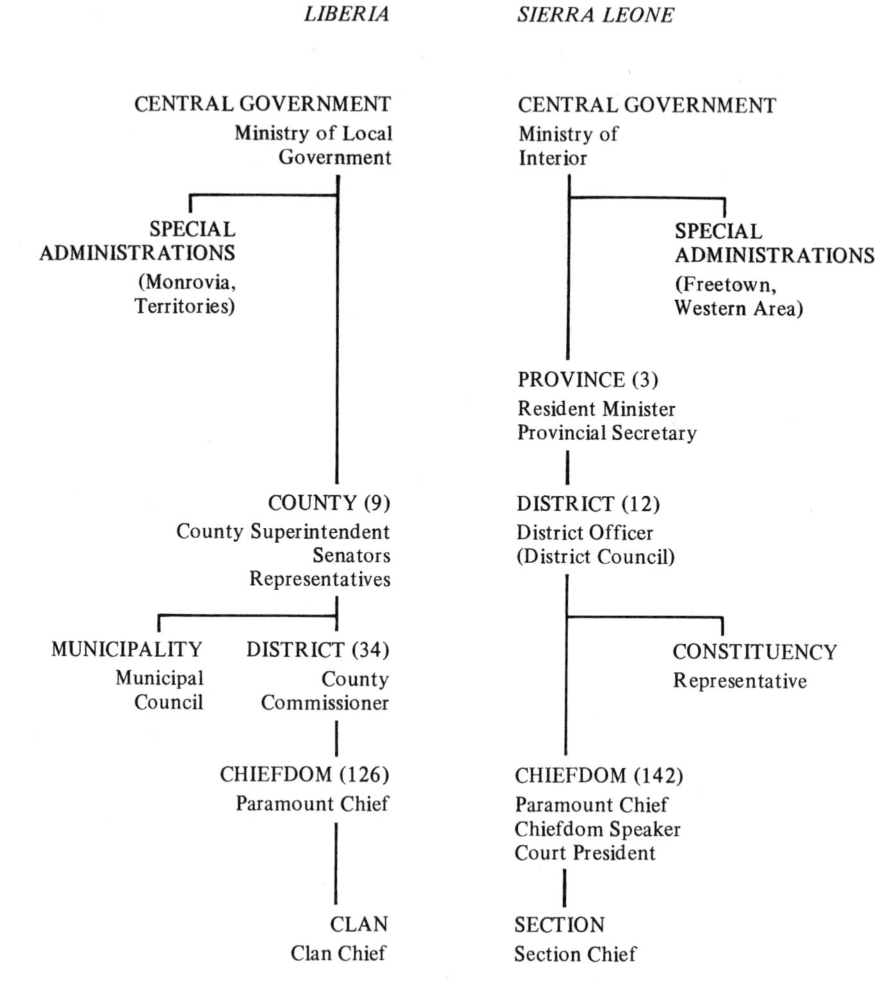

Notes

Local administrative divisions of roughly equivalent size and importance are placed opposite one another, with the number of units in each.

District Councils in Sierra Leone were suspended in 1967, and abolished in 1973.

Figure 1. The Formal Hierarchy of Local Administration.

and are reflected in divergences in local politics. The greater power of the Liberian centre is frequently apparent, though its more important feature is often, rather, its greater impermeability to peripheral pressures. By the same token, precisely because of the greater role of local factions in Sierra Leonean national politics, the 'centre' in Sierra Leone is often an extension of conflicts in which local politicians are themselves engaged; to Liberian local politicians, it is largely an external force. Yet because conflicts at the two levels are more directly relevant to one another in Sierra Leone than they are in Liberia, the Liberian periphery can maintain in some respects a greater autonomy from central penetration, and can make allocations locally which in Sierra Leone would be subject to central political pressure. The degree of local self-government in Liberia, especially in the hinterland Counties, is one of the most interesting and – to an observer fresh from its central politics – most surprising aspects of the whole political system.

The following sections will examine these themes, looking first at the base unit of local government in both countries – the chiefdom – and then at the linkages between local and central levels.

THE CHIEFDOM

There are at the time of writing some 126 chiefdoms in Liberia and 146 in Sierra Leone, varying in population from a few thousand people up to fifty thousand or more, and each governed by a Paramount Chief. They are divided in Sierra Leone into sections and in Liberia into clans, under a section or clan chief; the 'clan', confusingly, is a purely territorial unit with no kinship significance. Unlike many West African local administrations, in central Ghana for example or northern Nigeria, these chiefdoms can scarcely in any very useful way be described as 'traditional' units. They were, rather, created by the colonial and Liberian governments as part of the process of establishing control over the hinterland, and they differ widely in their degree of continuity with pre-colonial chieftaincies. The main factor determining their size and government has been administrative convenience. In Sierra Leone Mendeland, for example, the late nineteenth-century war chiefdoms were broken down into units which presented less of a threat to the colonial power.[1] In the Kpelle country of central Liberia, the small pre-conquest chiefdoms were lumped together into more manageable units.[2] In both countries chiefdoms have often been amalgamated in order to enable them to perform functions laid on them by the central government, and this practice continues in Liberia, though in Sierra Leone no changes have been made since independence.

This emphasis is necessary firstly to counteract the misleading impression of traditional continuity which terms such as 'Paramount Chief' are apt to give, and secondly to underline the fact that chiefdom politics cannot be divorced from relations with the centre. Chiefdoms gain their importance as political arenas from the prizes which they have to offer in a national political structure established in the present century, rather than on any particular continuity with the pre-colonial past. Only in parts of northern Sierra Leone does enough of the pre-colonial chiefdom structure survive to place any appreciable constraints on the behaviour expected of a chief, and this may help to explain why reactions against chiefly abuse of power have been greater there than in the south. Elsewhere, chiefs have to pay some attention to the norms of the indigenous society, especially the Poro, but it seems more accurate to regard them as secular administrators and politicians than as the 'natural leaders' of their people.

The most important prize allocated at the chiefdom level in both countries is the paramount chieftaincy itself. The question of who becomes chief, and how, thus not only indicates the chief's own position in the political structure, but also provides an entrée to most of the conflicts implicit in chiefdom politics. These can be compared in terms of the political base which candidates need in order to challenge for the chieftaincy, the resources which they mobilise in appeals both inside the chiefdom and beyond it, the form taken by the resulting campaign, and the overall balance of resources indicated in the outcome.

In Sierra Leone, the paramount chieftaincy is restricted to the members of specified 'chiefly families', of which there are between one and four in each chiefdom. Succession is not by heredity, but by an election from any number of qualified candidates, in which the voters are the 'Chiefdom Councillors' who are nominally elected by the taxpayers in the chiefdom.[3] In some chiefdoms, especially in the north, the chieftaincy is in principle rotated between the chiefly families, so that each gets its chance in turn, but such arrangements are apt to be disregarded in the stress of an election. The candidate's base in local society is thus provided mainly by family membership, and competition tends to be structured along family lines, with each qualified family putting forward its candidate. Fairly often, too, rival members of a family may stand against one another, or a family may ally itself with another against a common rival, rather than putting forward a candidate of its own. Controversy often arises over whether a particular candidate is qualified or not, and this has tended to increase since 1968 through attempts by local APC leaders, with central government support, to take over the chieftaincy. Such controversies were not so frequent under the SLPP because this was more closely allied with the chiefly elite, and in any case had scarcely any local organisation beyond that provided by the chiefs themselves.

In Liberia, by contrast, any chiefdom citizen can stand for election to the chieftaincy, and this term is generally interpreted to include not only natives of the chiefdom but also anyone owning a hut or other property on which he pays tax.[4] All chiefdom citizens, too, are entitled to vote, though in the absence of registers there is often dispute over who is a citizen and who is not. Family connections are thus not so critical in providing candidates, though the relatives of a well-established former chief will themselves be likely to have the status and economic leverage needed to challenge for the chieftaincy; this was certainly true of elections in 1972–3 in the Vai chiefdoms of Cape Mount/Garwula and Cape Mount/Porkpa.[5] Unlike Sierra Leone, though, self-made men who have built up a position of wealth and status may equally stand for the chieftaincy, as has happened in several of the Kpelle chiefdoms such as Bong/Panta and Bong/Kpai. Government employees favoured by the administration may also be encouraged to stand, the extreme case being that of Chief Dennis of Lofa/Bunde-Wubomai, one of Tubman's former household servants, who was in effect simply appointed by the President in 1966. The position of clan chief very often provides a base from which to challenge for the paramount chieftaincy.

These criteria reflect the local resources generated for chiefdom elections. In Liberia, each clan will tend (subject to his popularity and intra-clan factions) to support its own clan chief for the paramountcy, just as in Sierra Leone each chiefly family tends to have its supporters grouped in particular areas of the chiefdom; this is especially marked in amalgamated chiefdoms, such as Port Loko/Marampa-Masimera, where political conflict often follows the divisions between the formerly separate chiefdoms. This pattern of conflict tallies with the distribution of economic benefits, since a Paramount Chief can be expected to channel these to his own home area. Other local issues are mobilised whenever relevant. In the Sierra Leone diamond areas of Kono and Kenema/Lower Bambara, the tensions created by illicit diamond mining and the consequent influx of strangers generate resources for use in chiefdom as well as parliamentary elections.[6] This particular source of tension does not arise in Liberia, but analogous issues are drawn on in a very similar way. The Cape Mount/Porkpa chiefdom election of September 1972, for example, turned largely on the rivalry between the north and south of the chiefdom, and in particular on the construction of a road to the northern area which would have by-passed the main villages in the south. Personality is another obvious factor.

These local disputes are then related to resources generated outside, at District/County or national level. The connections which a candidate has at these levels may help him either through direct manipulation by the outside authorities, or because the voters themselves perceive them as a resource which will enable the candidate, if elected, to bring benefits to the chiefdom. To outside politicians, the chiefdom offers resources, economic or political, which are valuable to them and which they can gain in exchange for support for one of the local candidates. Despite the electoral rules for the recruitment of chiefs in both countries, which favour the resources implicit in local popularity, considerable scope exists for outside manipulation. In Liberia, the elections are held in some public place – the Commissioner's compound, a football field, or the village street – where the candidates stand side by side while their supporters line up behind them; the supervising authorities then check the credentials of the voters in each line, and this gives them some opportunity for weeding out disputed voters for the candidates whom they oppose. In Sierra Leone, rather greater opportunities exist through the selection of the Chiefdom Councillors; though nominally these are elected by the chiefdom taxpayers, I have found no record of any such election actually taking place, and in several recent cases the lists have allegedly been fixed by local factions in alliance with governing party politicians.[7] In Liberia, official intervention has reportedly diminished under the Tolbert administration, and chiefdom elections are now conducted by officials from the Electoral Commission in Monrovia who have few personal interests in chiefdom-level politics; in Sierra Leone, such intervention has increased.

The resources which local candidates can offer in exchange for outside support reflect the needs and interests of central or District/County level politicians. In Liberia, such politicians have very little need for chiefdom-level support in order to maintain themselves in office; to some extent, a County Superintendent may find himself in trouble if he fails to settle a chiefdom dispute, or a Representative may find local support useful in a bid for renomination by the TWP, but the effects are no more than marginal. Pay-offs to higher level politicians tend therefore to be couched in economic terms. In the Cape Mount/Porkpa election already referred to, several County officials were said to favour the candidate from the northern part of the chiefdom, since the new road which he used to generate local support would also have opened up virgin forest land in which the officials hoped to gain an interest; nonetheless, this candidate lost. In other cases, a candidate may have personal connections with an outside politician, as in the nearby chiefdom of Cape Mount/Garwula where the losing candidate was the cousin of a Senator, or the much more direct presidential intervention in Lofa/Bunde-Wubomai already noted. But since Liberian politicking is covert, and the resources involved are not of vital importance to either side, this external intervention is generally muted, and does not prevent officials or representatives from working with whoever is elected. Open competition at the chiefdom level can thus be combined with more closed forms of politics at the centre.

In Sierra Leone, there is a much more direct exchange of central influence for local political support. Under the rules for parliamentary elections, Representatives very often depended on the resources generated by chiefdom conflicts; in 1967, for example, the elections in Kenema Town and Kenema Central constituencies turned directly on the hotly disputed contest for the succession to the Kenema/Nongowa paramountcy.[8] When the party system converts victory in such an election into support for one national government or another, then the choice of factions at chiefdom level becomes vital to the exercise of central power. Milton Margai, with his loosely constructed central coalition, was able to stand aloof from such chiefdom disputes and recruit to his support whoever won them; Albert Margai sought more dependable allies than this system could produce, and his involvement in the Kenema/Nongowa dispute on the side which lost the two parliamentary seats in 1967 resulted in the return of two of the small group of southern Representatives whose hostility to him was decisive in preventing his re-election. Even though the electoral importance of chiefdom politics has diminished with the imposition of a single-party state in which candidates are chosen centrally, national politicians continue to seek to influence chiefdom elections in order to maintain their local base; indeed, the opportunities for this have increased. In Port Loko/Koya, home of the Agriculture Minister S. A. T. Koroma, an APC youth leader was elected Paramount Chief in 1973 despite protests that he was not even a member of a chiefly house.[9]

Campaign tactics in chieftaincy elections, except when these are preempted by outside intervention, are characteristically geared to the construction of a winning coalition from the discrete blocs of support created in each chiefdom by clan, family, native/stranger and other divisions. Each candidate seeks to expand his core support base by arranging alliances and offering side-payments to the controllers of other voting blocs.[10] Two Liberian cases will show the patterns, which are similar in Sierra Leone.[11] The election in Cape Mount/Garwula in 1973 was fought mainly on clan lines. The three principal candidates were Zuanneh Sherman from the Kiahun Clan, who had been acting Paramount Chief since the previous incumbent was pensioned off, Momo Golo, who had been Clan Chief of the Mano Bala Clan for the previous nineteen years, and the Zogbo Clan Chief Jimmy Gray; a few other candidates wanted to run, but were induced to stand down so as not to split the clan vote. Two clans in the five-clan chiefdom presented no candidate for the paramountcy, but had longstanding alliances, the Kiadiis with the Kiahuns, and the Kiazolus with the Mano Balas. That left Zuanneh Sherman and Momo Golo in the lead, with Jimmy Gray holding the balance between them; he stood down in Golo's favour, reportedly as a result of mediation by a Representative who was a close friend of Golo, and this more than offset the tacit support which Sherman received from his kinsman and namesake Senator Charles B. Sherman. Golo consequently won by some eighty votes in a turnout of about 2500, and Gray received his pay-off in the form of the clan chieftaincy of a large clan created by the amalgamation of the Mano Bala, Kiazolu and Zogbo Clans.

The election in Bong/Kpai in the same year was fought on rather different lines, since it had only two clans of which one, Waytwo, was much larger than the second, Wolota. There were initially four candidates, three of them from Waytwo: Madam Nowai Leemu, the clan chief and acting Paramount Chief, niece of a former paramount; Benjamin B. Greeves, who had been Paramount Chief no fewer than three times previously, and been deposed each time; Jerome Clarke, the primary school principal; and finally Charlie Toe, the Wolota Clan Chief, a self-made entrepreneur who owned a large farm and a couple of taxis. The County Superintendent was universally believed to favour Madam Nowai, and his influence induced the school principal to stand down in return for the refund of his expenses, some $200--300. The other three candidates went forward to the election, but when Greeves saw that his line was the shortest, he took his supporters over to Charlie Toe. Reasons given for this move range from his dislike of Madam Nowai to a straight cash payment of $300. Madam Nowai also lost support on the grounds that as a woman she could not enter the Poro Society bush where many community decisions were made; her rule as clan chief and acting paramount had not been popular, and she got most of her support from the Superintendent, a few outside landlords with plantations in the chiefdom, and two villages in the Wolota Clan which had local grievances against Charlie Toe. The first election was inconclusive, due to the confusion caused by Greeves' abrupt change, but Charlie Toe won the run-off by 1064 votes to 889.[12]

The winning candidate in this election, so far as I could calculate, spent comfortably over $1000 in gifts to village notables, food and drink for his supporters, and the hire of taxis to bring his voters to the poll. This sum is perhaps not very large, though it may be a considerable underestimate. Presumably, however, the economic and political rewards which the chieftaincy had to offer were enough to compensate him for the outlay. The wealth which a Paramount Chief gains from his office in either country is impossible to gauge at all accurately, since a high proportion of it comes from the exercise of his influence in ways which are informal and often illegal. In Sierra Leone, illegal exactions by chiefs have been a constant source of complaint for the last fifty years, most dramatically in the riots of 1955–6. In Liberia Chiefs have not enjoyed the same degree of independence or immunity from government punishment, but the same complaints are made. In both countries, the weakness of traditional constraints and obligations on the chieftaincy presumably helps to foster an extractive relationship between chiefs and people, which in turn may lead to rural violence.

It is however possible to compare the official emoluments of Paramount Chiefs, and to sketch some of the possibilities for making money on the side. The basis for calculating the official earnings is given in Table 4, though the figures are highly approximate since so much depends on variable fees, rents and commissions, and on the value of the rice which until 1973 made up a large part of the emoluments of a Liberian Paramount Chief. Despite the inadequacy of the figures, two points stand out. The first is the astonishing drop in the earnings of a Liberian Paramount Chief brought about by the shift in 1973 from payments in kind and commission to a regular salary; the effect of this measure in reducing chiefs to further dependence on the centre was recognised in the chiefdoms at the time, even though its implications had not fully sunk in. In the chiefdoms which I visited in 1973, I found a general awareness that these changes had been made, and that payments in kind to the Paramount Chief were no longer required. Secondly, the salary of a Sierra Leone Paramount Chief is much greater than that of his Liberian equivalent, even though before 1973 their total emoluments did not differ very markedly.

For the Liberian chief, the main opportunities for further enrichment come from the allocation of labour. In a labour-short economy, the chief is often in the best position to get people to work on his farms. A well-established chief may be able simply to order people to work for him, in return for which he will be expected to provide food and occasional gifts; and any chief can apply rewards and constraints which make work for him more attractive than for other

Table 4. *Officially Recognised Payments to Paramount Chiefs*

Chiefdom size	Sierra Leone	Liberia before 1973	Liberia after 1973
1500 huts/taxpayers	(small)	(small–medium)	(small–medium)
Government salary	Le1500	nil	$800–900
Commission on taxes	150	$825	nil
Rice (@ 1973 prices)	nil	$1200	nil
Court fees	few	†	†
Rents	*	nil	nil
Total	Le1650+	$2025+	$800–900+
3000 huts/taxpayers	(medium)	(large)	(large)
Government salary	Le2200	nil	$800–900
Commission on taxes	300	$1650	nil
Rice (@ 1973 prices)	nil	1200	nil
Court fees	few	†	†
Rents	*	nil	nil
Total	Le2500+	$2850+	$800–900+
6000 huts/taxpayers	(large)		
Government salary	Le2800		
Commission on taxes	600		
Court fees	few		
Rents	*		
Total	Le3400+		

* Rents: Sierra Leone chiefs retain one-third of rents on chiefdom land leased to strangers.
† Court fees: Liberian chiefs charge a fee of about $10 per case; in Sierra Leone, most such fees have been taken over by the Court President.

Notes

Government salary: in Sierra Leone, this varies with the size of the chiefdom, and is paid half from the central government, and half from the chiefdom treasury; in Liberia, it is paid by the central government; there was an even divergence of opinion among informants in the chiefdoms over whether the new salary is $800 or $900 a year.

Commission: Sierra Leone chiefs retain 10c of the personal tax of Le3.00; Liberian chiefs until 1973 retained 5% of the Hut Tax of $6.00, and 2½% of the Education Tax of $10.00.

Rice: Liberian chiefs until 1973 received 160 100lb bags of rice from the chiefdom; this is valued at the 1973 price of $8 per bag, though the price in previous years had been about half as much.

landowners. He may also be able to gain preferential access to government services like tree nurseries or agricultural advisers, and to exact payments for services like his signature on land sale certificates. In the past chiefs have received cash payments from foreign concessions such as the Firestone rubber plantation for the compulsory recruitment of labour for work outside the chiefdom.[13]

Sierra Leone chiefs have greater opportunities, and more often possess signs of conspicuous consumption such as motor cars. The fact that they are much less easily deposed than Liberian ones strengthens their ability to exact services from their people, and they also have access to chiefdom treasuries and (until their abolition in 1973) to District Councils. The Auditor-General's reports on District Council and chiefdom finances are filled with cries of despair which indicate that control of these accounts is in practice impossible; all manner of expense allowances, loans and so forth serve effectively as means of increasing the chief's income.[14] Nor are chiefs subject to much effective control by the District Officers, who may be taking advantage of the same abuses themselves.[15] The chiefs in the diamond areas come into a category of their own, since they can gain financially from the influx of strangers, and in many ways exchange their powers of local regulation for a cut of the wealth being extracted from their territory.[16] Other forms of economic development also profit the Sierra Leone chief. In the iron ore chiefdom of Port Loko/Marampa-Masimera, Delco makes an annual payment to chiefdom funds, increased in 1973 from Le10,000 to 20,000; this does not go directly to the Paramount Chief, but he has a considerable say in its distribution.[17] In urban chiefdoms such as Kenema/Nongowa, which includes the town of Kenema, the Paramount Chief's right to a third of the rent on buildings leased to strangers brings in a handsome sum, and helps to account for the intensity of political conflict in the chiefdom.[18] On a smaller scale, even a rice project manned by Communist Chinese helps to subsidise the chief, since the crop goes to him for distribution. The Liberian chief has few such opportunities.

The superior status of chieftaincy in Sierra Leone which this suggests is confirmed when one looks at the patterns of recruitment, both to the chieftaincy and from it. In Liberia, a paramount chiefdom is the highest position to which an unlettered man can aspire. A high proportion of Liberian chiefs have no formal education, including three of the four chiefs in Grand Cape Mount County and four of the eleven in Bong County in 1973, as well as probably the most powerful Paramount Chief in the country, Tamba Taylor of Lofa/Kissi. In Sierra Leone, except in backward areas such as Koinadugu District, it is already beyond an illiterate's grasp. This is partly because the chiefly families have been the earliest beneficiaries of western education, but partly also because chieftaincy is a prize important enough to attract competitors who would not consider it worthy of them in Liberia.

In Liberia, the central-dominant system has drawn educated people away from the chiefdoms, and into jobs in the County administration and Monrovia. It is symptomatic of this that Cape Mount, where three-quarters of the chiefs are uneducated, has the oldest tradition of tribal education in Liberia. The attitude persists that chieftaincy is for the unlettered tribespeople, and even a village schoolmaster rarely sees his advancement as lying by that road. This attitude is not so marked in the hinterland, where there is a greater tendency to see advancement as lying in identification with one's local community rather than in the lure of Monrovia; in Bong/Kpai election of 1973, as noted above, the local primary school principal stood, though hesitantly and unsuccessfully, for the office. For the ambitious, a paramount chieftaincy is attractive not so much for its own sake, but rather as a means of acquiring a status which can in turn be exchanged for a position outside the chiefdom, in particular for a seat in the House of Representatives. In Bong County, four of the six Representatives are former Paramount Chiefs; in Cape Mount, where there is a much larger number of educated tribal men contesting for seats in the House, there is nonetheless a convention that one of the seats should be reserved for the traditional element in the community, and the ambition to succeed to this was one of the main motivating factors for at least some of the candidates in chiefdom elections in 1972–3. One young graduate who became a Paramount Chief in Nimba County exchanged this almost immediately for a seat in the House of Representatives. Certainly not all Paramount Chiefs want to make the change; some have established positions in their own chiefdoms which they would not abandon for the uncertainties of a place on the fringes of the establishment in Monrovia. But on the other hand it would be unthinkable for a Representative or even a County Commissioner (in charge of a small Liberian District) to step down to a paramount chieftaincy.

The situation is reversed in Sierra Leone, where both the British legacy of indirect rule and the recruitment of the central political leadership from the chiefly families of the Protectorate have helped to give the Paramount Chief a status to which even educated hinterlanders may aspire. Not all of them do so, and most chieftaincy contestants are local level politicians whose horizons do not stretch far beyond their own chiefdoms; but an SLPP Cabinet Minister and Government Chief Whip won the important Bo/Kakua chiefdom in 1966, and the local APC Representative contested unsuccessfully the not specially important chiefdom of Tonkolili/Kunike in 1970. Thus a paramount chieftaincy in Sierra Leone continues to be a prize which is comparable in status, and superior in security, to those to be gained at the central level.

A Paramount Chief in Sierra Leone holds office until death or – much more rarely – deposition. In the twelve years following independence only eighteen Paramount Chiefs were deposed,[19] most of them following the APC's accession to power in 1968, and cases of voluntary retirement or resignation are almost unheard of. Chiefs therefore stay in office for a very long time; in 1969–70, for example, 19 of the 142 Paramount Chiefs had been in office since 1940 or earlier, and a further 21 since 1941–50; of the rest, 53 had been installed between 1951 and 1960, and 49 since independence in 1961.[20] I have no equivalent figures for Liberia; there, however, Paramount Chiefs are regularly pensioned off, and can be deposed or suspended without difficulty by the President, the Minister of Local Government or the County Superintendent. The decisions of the lower officials may be appealed to the President, but a Liberian chief is unlikely to have anything approaching their political influence. From 1975, moreover, a drastic change is due to take place since Paramount Chiefs then become liable for re-election every four years, further increasing the insecurity of their position. This change was announced in 1973 by executive fiat, without involving any of the political repercussions which would follow from such a move in Sierra Leone.

The political influence of Paramount Chiefs depends both on the extent of their authority within the chiefdom and on the opportunities which the office gives them for deploying resources outside it. Within the chiefdom, the institutional and many of the practical constraints on the power of the chief are greater in Sierra Leone than in Liberia. Though this appears to run counter to the pattern that Sierra Leonean Paramount Chiefs are more powerful than their Liberian counterparts, it is due both to the way in which the central dependence of Liberian chiefs insures them to some extent against local opposition, and to the central government's need in Sierra Leone for some countervailing power at the chiefdom level to balance the chief's influence outside it. The main institutional constraints on a Sierra Leone Paramount Chief within his own chiefdom are the pressure of two offices, the Chiefdom Speaker and the Court President, which may provide alternative foci for influence. The Chiefdom Speaker is the Paramount Chief's deputy and chief of staff, and though formally elected is often effectively appointed by the chief; however, he may be opposed to the chief, or if allied with him may have been chosen to represent another section within the chiefdom.[21] The Court President has taken over one of the chief's most profitable and influential functions, and his presence is the reason most often given for the decline in the power of chiefs. The office was at first elective, but since 1963 has been subject to appointment by the Prime Minister,[22] a clear indication of the shift in resources to the centre after independence. Though the Prime Minister or President is nominally advised on appointments by a three-man committee of officials, the post has in practice been used quite simply for political patronage, especially in chiefdoms where the Paramount is opposed to the governing party. The resulting decline in the quality of justice has enabled chiefs to regain, informally, some of their previous judicial functions.

This political intervention in the local court system serves to re-emphasise the importance of the central political system for local politics. By far the greater part of the differences in chiefdom politics between the two countries spring from the rules imposed from the centre, rather than from any appreciable variations in the purely local situation. The rules of local politics perceived at the chiefdom level in Liberia are fairly simple and consistent. The chief who diligently collects his taxes and responds to the administrative requirements of the central government and his local Superintendent has little to fear, and unless he is very inept can rely on central support should troubles arise in his chiefdom. The most that he will have to do is to ensure that he does not become too dependent on a particular section of the administration to be able to adapt to the limited range of changes that the system may produce; there may be a fight between a Senator and a Superintendent, and a disgraced official may bring down a chief with whom he was particularly friendly, as Superintendent Gbarbea in Bong County did in 1968; a new Superintendent or a new President may make demands which call for a change of style from the chief. But on the whole this is not too difficult: there is only one party and one administration, and the possibility of it changing or being overthrown is not taken into account in the calculation of political strategies at the local level. Even the potential tension between the chief's links with the administration and those with his own people comes into the open for the most part only when a new chief is being elected, and the local people receive a resource which is otherwise denied them. This may change, and the chief's position become harder to manage, when the promised system of regular four-yearly elections comes into effect in 1975.

The Sierra Leone Paramount Chief is in a much trickier position. The potential inconsistencies between his roles as leader of his people, administrative agent, and supporter of the party or regime currently in power are far greater than anything which the Liberian Paramount Chief has to face.[23] There is not one set of rules. There are a number of different sets of rules, and the chief has to reconcile them as best he may, or shift from one to another. The tensions in the chief's relationship with his people are in any case greater than in Liberia: the riots against chiefs in northern Sierra Leone in 1955–6 are the clearest example of local pressures of a kind which have not appeared in Liberia. But the situation is vastly complicated by party politics, and the possibility of abrupt extraneous change in the central government. Chiefs as administrative agents have to act in concert with the government of the day. After independence, and increasingly as governments became unpopular in some area of the country, this meant that they had to identify themselves with the government and party in power, and harass the opposition. If they did not do so, then the government – through such devices as the appointment of Court Presidents or the encouragement of unruly local factions – could intensify their local conflicts as well as cutting off other allocations. Barrows has shown very clearly how the incidence of violence at the chiefdom level in Kenema District rose and fell with the opportunities available to its instigators for appealing to the central government.[24] Paramount Chief Dudu Bona of Kono/Nimikoro, a well-known SLPP sympathiser, was physically assaulted in 1972 by a group of APC youths led by his own Court President.[25] Yet the attachment to the centre on which the chief then has to rely becomes a liability when the central ruling group is changed by forces over which he has no control. By far the greatest number of depositions of Paramount Chiefs have resulted from the changes in the central government in 1967–8. Most of these were in the north, where the popularity of the APC both led the SLPP government to use the chiefs as its agents in suppressing the opposition, and made it easy for the APC to dispose of them when it came to power in its turn.

But the Paramount Chief in Sierra Leone has something to fight back with. The central government can depose any chief if it is determined enough to do so, but this is a long-drawn out process. The chiefs who incurred the anger of the APC by supporting the SLPP government in the north were not actually deposed until two and a half years after the return to civilian rule. Meanwhile, the government itself depends on the chiefs as its local administrative agents. A chief who is prepared to recant and produce at least a token display of loyalty to the governing party can generally retain his office, unless he occupies the local fief of a powerful and hostile minister. The former SLPP minister who became Paramount Chief of Bo/Kakua remained in office until his death in 1973, despite evidence that he had been involved in several corrupt deals,[26] and even after six years of APC rule many chiefs remained whose preference for the SLPP was scarcely concealed.

The greatest difference of all between Paramount Chiefs in the two countries lies in the opportunities open to the Sierra Leonean chief for political influence beyond his own chiefdom. The Sierra Leone chief, first of all, is often closely related to the group of politicians – in the SLPP especially, but also to some extent the APC – from which the national leadership is drawn. He is far more likely therefore to have direct access to the centre through a relative or political ally in high office, and to be able to use his contacts to obtain allocations for his own chiefdom without needing to pass through intermediaries at District or Provincial level. This influence was greatest during the period of fairly open electoral competition before 1967, when the chief might be an important factor in a Minister or Representative's chances of re-election. The chief also has some opportunities for direct central participation on his own account, especially under the provision for one Paramount Chief from each District to sit in the House of Representatives. In practice, the Paramount Chief Representatives have always supported the government of the day: any other stance would be foolhardy for men who are both elected Representatives and government administrative agents. Many of them have played a very limited role in the House. However, several of them have served as Cabinet Ministers without Portfolio, Paramount Chief Koker of Bo/Bagbo is Chairman of the Sierra Leone Produce Marketing Board, and Paramount Chief Kai-Kai of Pujehun acted as Prime Minister in 1973 during S. I. Koroma's absence abroad.

With a very few exceptions, Liberian chiefs have none of these opportunities for exercising political influence at the centre. Several of them, certainly, have become Representatives, giving up their chieftaincies in order to do so; but this provides little entrée to the closed circles of the central elite, and a legislative position holds little power in itself. Most chiefs are subordinate to their local County Commissioner, and their political horizons do not stretch beyond the County Superintendent. In the whole of Liberia, there are probably only two exceptions to this rule, Tamba Taylor of Lofa/Kissi and Thomas Kollie of Lofa/Gbandi, and their positions are interesting enough to be worth examining more closely.

The two have a great deal in common, besides being close friends and allies. They govern neighbouring chiefdoms in north-west Lofa County on the Guinea and Sierra Leone frontiers, and they belong to small ethnic groups, the Kissis and the Gbandis, all of whose people within Liberia belong to their chiefdoms. Both chiefdoms are fairly highly developed for the cultivation of cocoa, coffee and, most recently, rice. Neither chief comes from any well-known local family, and so far as one can trust accounts given in 1973 of their election during the 1950s, both seem to have gained office primarily through the support of the administration. Kollie had been a government interpreter, and Taylor stood against the brother of a previous Paramount Chief who had been powerful and independent enough to excite central distrust. Once in office, both proved to be active developmentalists, and were able both to secure benefits for their chiefdoms – a road, a school, a new market – and to strengthen their contacts with the centre. Chief Kollie became Chairman of the Lofa County caucus of the True Whig Party when the hinterland government was reformed in 1964, and one of Chief Taylor's sons was reared in Monrovia by the then Vice-President Tolbert. Foya in Kissi Chiefdom was chosen for the government's most ambitious agricultural development scheme, with a 2500-acre rice project.

These contacts enable the two chiefs effectively to by-pass the County Administration and work directly with Monrovia. Both the local Representative and the County Commissioner are their nominees – the Commissioner was formerly Chief Taylor's clerk – and the County Superintendent, though his formal authority is acknowledged, has little to do with the administration of the area. The two chiefs are even able to use their central connections and Chief Kollie's role as TWP Chairman to challenge his allocations at the County level, for instance over the spending of Rally funds and the siting of the proposed new road from Monrovia to Lofa County. In Monrovia, Chief Taylor's son is second-in-charge of the government purchasing agency, and Chief Kollie's nephew is Assistant Minister for Rural Development.

These two chiefs, it must be said again, are very much the exception, but some useful conclusions can be drawn from them. Firstly, they are in no way independent of the central government; it is their very closeness to the centre which has enabled them to build up their position. Secondly, however, they have used their local dynamism to create resources which are valuable to the centre; this, added to the fact that they represent small tribes which present no threat in national terms, must account for their political importance compared with other chiefs. Thirdly, Taylor and Kollie are able to transact a *direct* exchange of resources with the centre, by-passing the intermediaries who are the main beneficiaries of central–local exchange in other parts of Liberia.

In neither country is the position of Paramount Chiefs constant, and in both, the resources at their disposal have ostensibly declined. In Sierra Leone, there has been a shift away from the local level as a whole since independence and especially since 1967; the 1967 election and its aftermath made it clear both that the role of Paramount Chiefs in allocating parliamentary seats was declining, especially in the north and Kono, and that the interests of central groups in gaining or maintaining power were too great for them to allow its allocation to be undertaken from the periphery. It could equally be argued that the exceptional position which the chiefs held during the 1950s carried the seeds of its own decay, because the rules governing their political participation and their administrative roles were, once it came to the point, irreconcilable. Electoral politics may even, in the long run, have weakened the chiefs by destroying the autonomy of the chiefdom, opening its factional conflicts to penetration from outside and encouraging actors other than the chief to establish linkages with national political brokers. Moreover, when politics is conducted largely as a constant-sum contest for local office, the chiefdom as a whole may be the loser, gratuitously fragmenting itself in order to provide support for central-level actors who have little to offer in exchange.

In this light, the establishment of APC hegemony at the centre – by no means yet secure – at least enables Paramount Chiefs to fall back on their old administrative functions. The position of the chiefs in this respect is secure, at least to the extent that no alternative to them as agents of local government has been seriously suggested. Nor does the central government place very heavy demands on them as agents of development or party activists. As Barrows suggests, they are being not so much displaced as supplemented by officials at the District and Provincial levels, carrying out new tasks for which the Paramount Chief is redundant.[27]

In Liberia, the decline of the Paramount Chief is in some ways much more clearly marked. Two vital rule changes under the Tolbert government have cut at his financial position and his security of tenure, reducing him to a paid (and not very well paid) official subject to quadriennial re-election. These moves can be seen partly as an imposition of further control from the centre, but also as an appeal over the head of the Paramount Chief from the centre to the chiefdom-level taxpayer. His tax has been reduced, he no longer has to produce rice for the chief, and he has greater opportunities for controlling the chief through elections. But since the relations between centre and periphery are potentially so much more fluid in Liberia than in Sierra Leone, these changes may cut both ways. It may be possible for chiefs resentful of their treatment by government to appeal more directly to their own people (with whom they have no longer such an extractive relationship), and the same trend may be fortified by the more regular elections which were due to be instituted in 1975.

THE INTERMEDIARY ROLE

There is a sense in which anyone is an intermediary who is involved in any shift of resources from one level to another. The chief is an intermediary between his own people and government, just as the President is one whenever he goes on a provincial tour, or receives a local delegation in his office. In this section, I will be concerned mostly with those actors who operate above the chiefdom but below the central level, or who move regularly between the two. I prefer 'intermediary' to the alternative term 'broker', because it takes much less for granted. Brokerage implies that a regular process of exchange is taking place, in which the local level possesses resources which the centre requires, and is independent enough to bargain over the terms on which they will be offered; the broker is then the man with a foot in each camp who fixes the terms of exchange, taking his cut as he does so, and thus builds up a personal position not fully dependent on either level. This is appropriate to some aspects of the relationship, especially to the formation of alliances between local factions and central parties or other competing groups, but it does not cover the relationship between a monopolistic central power and a local level which has little scope for bargaining. This may be a relationship simply of central control, or else one of patronage, in which selected local actors are admitted to a share of the benefits on terms laid down at the centre. There are other possible forms of the relationship which do not require even intermediaries, such as conflict between the two levels or the local arena's withdrawal from contact with the centre, but these have not been attempted since the resistance to the initial imposition of central control.

Despite the differences in political and administrative structure between Liberia and Sierra Leone, there are two sets of formal intermediary roles in each country which can conveniently be grouped together for comparison. These are firstly the appointed political and administrative leadership, represented by the County Superintendent in Liberia and the Resident Minister, the Provincial Secretary and the District Officer in Sierra Leone, together with the administrative apparatus over which they preside; and secondly the agencies of local representation provided by Senators and Representatives in Liberia, and Representatives in Sierra Leone, with the structures of support on which they rely. Though this distinction is by no means a clear one, it makes rather more sensc than the conventional dichotomy between 'party' and 'government', especially as the party systems of the two countries are so different. In addition, there are in each country opportunities for informal intermediaries and for direct central involvement in local politics.

In Sierra Leone, the first of these categories can perhaps only by courtesy be referred to as one of leadership positions at all, since a variety of factors have combined to reduce the influence which can be exercised at Province or District level.[28] These include the division between the District and the Province, the division between 'administrative' and 'political' roles represented at its clearest by the duplication of Provincial Secretary and Regional Minister, and the bypassing of both levels by Paramount Chiefs and especially by Representatives who operate direct with Freetown. The position of Regional Minister was created in 1961 in order to provide a channel for conflicts such as chieftaincy palavers, demands for development projects, and disputes within the local governing party. Unlike either the Provincial Secretary or the District Officer, the Regional Minister generally has some political links with his area, and serves for several years at a time. He is usually the Representative for a constituency in the Province, and carries the political weight of a middle to lower ranking minister. He provides no real equivalent to the Liberian Superintendent, however, since he does not direct the provincial administration, and the local party network is too fragmented to provide him with an alternative organisational base: any attempt to use it as such would arouse the hostility of more powerful ministers in Freetown whose own fiefs this would threaten. The Province, too, with a population ranging from seven hundred thousand to a million, is too large an area for the Regional Minister to make much of a mark. His functions thus extend little beyond conflict mediation, and he can easily be by-passed by delegations going straight to Freetown.

The Provincial Secretary and the District Officer are both civil service appointments, direct heirs to the administrative hierarchy of the colonial regime. For a few years after independence, colonial officials stayed on as Provincial Secretaries and sometimes DOs, being succeeded by a generation of Creole officials who have now in most cases been replaced by hinterlanders. These generally specialise in provincial administration, moving around from one District or Province to another, but as potential political intermediaries they suffer crippling disadvantages. Their civil service role inhibits them from performing the transactions in which political management largely consists, and they are poorly placed to establish any powerful bargaining position through either central influence or local contacts. They are expected to promote the interests of the government of the day – they had for instance to press Albert Margai's unpopular proposals for a single-party state[29] – but they have not received the corresponding central support which is found in systems where the local administrative boss is effectively the ruler's representative. Hence they cannot afford to offend a Minister or Representative whose constituency lies in the District, and this in turn affects their local standing, leading to criticisms of their failure to exercise effective control over chiefdom finances.[30] The 'complete lack of integrity on the part of many District Officers' has itself been the subject of outspoken criticism.[31] District Officers are only rarely posted to their own Districts of origin, and the reason given to the author by one high official in the Ministry of Interior, that chiefs would complain about being placed under someone who had been brought up as their inferior, indicates a further weakness in their position, which can be undercut by the chiefs' access to central government. Finally, they are transferred so rapidly from post to post that they never have a chance to become established local authority figures; the average length of stay in one post for a District Officer since independence has been about ten months.[32]

The position is very different in Liberia, where these roles are combined in a single official who has both unmistakably political functions and direct control over the County administration. There is a Superintendent in charge of each of the nine Counties,[33] and of the five coastal Territories which (largely for historical reasons) are administered separately. These are appointed directly by the President, and often have personal links and loyalties to him; all but two of the County Superintendents, for instance, were replaced by Tolbert within a year of his taking office. Usually they are appointed from officials who have made their career at the central level, though occasionally a local official is moved up to the

Superintendency. But although he is appointed from the centre, he is almost always a native of the County which he governs, and is expected to have some personal identification with it; of the nine Superintendents in 1973, only White of Grand Gedeh was not of local origin. The Superintendent thus embodies the tension between central and local linkages.

The Superintendent's ultimate dependence is on the centre, and this is reflected in the amount of his time – often more than half of it – which an ambitious Superintendent spends in Monrovia, and in the assiduity with which he waits on the President during his visits to the County. After President Tolbert started making surprise inspections of government offices in Monrovia, Superintendent Sumo Jones of Lofa County followed suit in his County capital, imposing fines of up to $50 on any official who was late for work.[34] This was a very clear exchange of local popularity for central favour, and was recognised as such at both levels. Superintendent Anderson of Maryland, a Tubman appointee in Tubman's home County, evidently felt the need to do the same as a gesture of deference to the Tolbert administration, but his fines of $5 were far less draconian.[35]

At the same time, a Superintendent needs to maintain local connections in order to meet the expectations of the central government and, if possible, build up a local reputation. He must keep on good terms with local influentials, especially with Senators whose political connections are usually much better than his own; he must seek to resolve local disputes, since any embarrassment which these cause to the government will certainly be visited on him; and he must be able to show results for whatever is the government's – or President's – current preoccupation. When President Tolbert threatened in August 1973 to dismiss any Superintendent who had not collected all arrears of taxes by the end of the year, the Superintendents in turn made the same threat to their local County Commissioners, tax collectors, and chiefs.[36] The National Fund-Raising Rally similarly required them to make local exactions in order to prove their central loyalty; and in a rather more constructive way, the President's call for self-sufficiency in rice production and the construction of feeder roads produced corresponding efforts from the more ambitious and dynamic Superintendents. The central focus of Liberian government thus produces greater opportunities both for exactions and for developmental impetus than exist in Sierra Leone, where the corresponding linkages are fragmented and blurred.

Though the Superintendent is one of the most important agents of central–local linkage in Liberia, he does not control them, since he can always be bypassed either by Senators and Representatives or by direct appeals to the President. In the coastal Counties, he has to tread warily in anything which affects the interests of any big local family with a place in the national elite. In the hinterland, the sensitivity of the Superintendency is intensified by the fact that this is one of the very few positions which enable a hinterlander to build up a local political base. As a result, the position is highly precarious. It may lead on to a fairly assured position as a Representative or perhaps a Minister, or else – indeed more often – end in dismissal, followed by obscurity or a slow climb back to favour.

The history of the hinterland Superintendents appointed since 1964 is therefore particularly instructive. The first batch, including James Gbarbea in Bong County and Robert Kennedy in Lofa, were recruited from educated young men who had gone back to their home areas to work as schoolmasters or minor government officials. Their sudden elevation to power was balanced by the selection of Americo-Liberian Senators with long experience of Bong and Lofa to keep an eye on them. They and the Nimba Superintendent were all dismissed in 1968, ostensibly because of involvement in the Farnbulleh affair of that year, which intensified President Tubman's suspicion of political activity in the hinterland.[37] In fact no evidence of complicity was ever presented, neither Gbarbea nor Kennedy was very popular locally, and their fall was due as much to the manoeuvring of local Senators as to national events. Both went without government jobs for the rest of the Tubman administration. Under Tolbert, Gbarbea had a brief period as Minister of Lands and Mines before joining the staff of a mining company, and Kennedy has restarted from lower down the central pyramid as Assistant Minister for Labour, Youth and Sports.

Their replacements, Korkoyah in Bong and Ballayan in Lofa, were promoted within the local hierarchy from the posts of County Inspector and County Attorney. Evidently taking fright from the experience of their predecessors, these took refuge in the contrary failing of inactivity, and were dismissed shortly after Tolbert's takeover for their 'inability to reflect the image of Government in the County'.[38] Korkoyah died shortly afterwards, and Ballayan retired to private legal practice.

Tolbert's appointees were much more central in their career patterns. Sumo Jones in Lofa was a security and immigration expert, and Harry Greaves in Bong, though an accountant by training, was Assistant Minister of Defense and had been an aide to Tolbert as Vice-President. Jones had been out of Lofa for many years, while Greaves had never even lived in Bong, having been born in Grand Bassa to Bong parents, and brought up by an Americo-Liberian notable. Both therefore viewed their career prospects in essentially central terms, though Greaves (much more than Jones) built up something of a local base by the vigour with which he defended Bong County interests and promoted local government projects. He even protested vocally to the President against Senator Frank Tolbert's attempt to transfer part of Bong County to Montserrado.[39]

This emphasis on local origins in the Superintendent is even more marked in the large though lowly paid County administration. The County headquarters is staffed by a mass of officials: County Inspector and County Attorney, Commissioners for Lands, for Labour and for Immigration, Judges for the Traffic Court and the Debt Court, with attendant Sheriffs, Magistrates, Registrars, Coroners and Notaries Public, Information Officers, Supervisors of Schools, and so forth. These officials perform linkage roles not so much through their designated duties, which are often slight, as through the opportunities which their jobs provide for local patronage. In Liberia as in the United States, the President's power of appointment to executive offices is delegated at the local level through the convention of Senatorial courtesy. Applications to the President for jobs in a County administration are generally referred by him to the Senators, who may also consult the Superintendent, the Representatives, and other influentials in the local TWP hierarchy. Though this is an obvious source of senatorial influence, it is doubtful whether Senators need it for political support. Most Senators are well enough established not to do so, and the election of a new one is not accompanied by any spate of nominations to the County administration.

Local recruitment also helps to maintain some local identity with government, and to mitigate – though not remove – exploitation by officials. In Cape Mount County, 86% of government jobs in 1973 were held by native Cape Mountainians, while in Lofa County the figure was 97% for Lofa citizens.[40] Lofa is exceptional among hinterland counties for its high number of educated citizens, due largely to mission education and especially to the Anglican secondary school at Bolahun, founded in 1924. Cape Mount County, where the episcopal secondary school at Robertsport was founded in 1878, has a similar pre-eminence among coastal counties. In Bong County, the proportion of locals in the County administration in 1973 was only 40%, though many of the 'strangers' had spent most of their lives in Bong County. Localism goes all the way down, so that County Commissioners (in Cape Mount and Lofa, though not so much in Bong) are generally natives of the District which they administer. To an appreciable extent, therefore, the inaccessibility of the central government is balanced by the openness of the local administration, in terms both of recruitment prospects for educated hinterlanders and of identification with the political system. One corollary of this is that movement between the county and central hierarchies is very slight, except at the level of the Superintendent. The only such case which I encountered was that of Alfred Kollie, a former County Commissioner in Lofa County, who became Co-ordinator for Rural Development in the Ministry of Local Government.

The Sierra Leone system, with an articulated civil service structure in place of the Liberian practice of individual appointments to specific posts, allows much greater opportunities for movement between central and local levels. Nonetheless a high proportion of interior posts are filled by hinterlanders, while Creoles tend to remain in Freetown. The problem of maintaining a balance between central control and local involvement in District administration has not been solved, since the solution inherited from the colonial government – the District Council – has finally been judged a failure. The District Councils were established in 1945, with a mixture of Paramount Chiefs and elected members. During the 1950s, and for a few years after independence, they took over responsibility for a great many projects, including schools and local roads. They suffered, however,

Table 5. *Senior Provincial Government Officials*

Sierra Leone

Provincial Commissioners and Secretaries, District Officers/Commissioners, by Province of origin

	Jan. 1963	*Jan. 1968*	*Sept. 1973*
Foreign	5	0	0
Western Area	6	5	2
Northern Province	3	2	6
Eastern Province	1	5	2
Southern Province	0	4	7
Total	15	16	17

Liberia

County and Territory Superintendents, Provincial Commissioners (1964 only)

(*a*) by ethnic group:

	Jan. 1964	*Jan. 1968*	*Sept. 1973*
Americo-Liberian	6	5	6
Tribal: coastal Counties	4	3	5
Tribal: hinterland Counties	0	3	3
Total	10	11	14

(*b*) by County of origin:

	Jan. 1964	*Jan. 1968*	*Sept. 1973*
Montserrado	1	0	2
Other coastal Counties	9	8	9
Hinterland Counties	0	3	3
Total	10	11	14

Notes and Sources

Sierra Leone names as for Table 3; Liberia names as for Table 1; information on origins from personal informants. The breakdown of ethnic origins for coastal Liberians must be treated with reserve.

from a lack of both financial and political autonomy, and never managed to establish themselves as independent centres for resource allocation.[41] Financially, they depended on central government grants in aid, and 'precepts' levied on each chiefdom. The chiefdom precepts were generally years in arrears, and the central funds could be cut off from a Council which showed signs of political recalcitrance; in the early 1960s, Sir Milton Margai starved the Kono District Council until enough of the opposition members had been brought over to give the SLPP a majority on it.[42] Politically, the Councils tended to act as extensions either downwards of government directives – for instance in passing resolutions calling for a one-party state in 1966[43] – or upwards of disputes between chiefdoms, especially over the allocation of benefits.[44] The NRC replaced the elected councils by Management Committees, which the APC government maintained until it abolished the Councils altogether in 1972.[45] Their functions were handed over to the local branches of central government agencies.

Representative roles differ from the appointive ones in that nominally they are allocated from the periphery. In practice, though on balance they are more likely than administrative ones to reflect local choice, they vary markedly both in the degree of central co-option and in the structure and composition of the group which makes the effective allocation at the local level.

Until about 1969, Sierra Leone was quite exceptional among African states in the extent to which the local resources at the candidate's disposal, expressed through voting, outweighed both party nomination and central co-option. This was especially true of the SLPP which, having very little party organisation either at central or at constituency level, relied for candidates on men who possessed their own local linkages through which to get out the vote and maintain support. Inevitably, such candidates tended to be local authority figures, since these alone possessed support networks which did not require any formal political organisation. Because of the intense chiefdom disputes referred to in the last section, and the low level of social and economic change, and correspondingly of political awareness, in most areas outside Freetown and Kono, these networks were frequently based on rivalries within and between chiefdoms. Even in Freetown, the SLPP maintained a similar approach through candidates such as Kandeh Bureh, the Temne tribal headman, or M. S. Mustapha, a Moslem Creole, who had their own analogous support structures. Within its limitations of elite leadership, this system offered considerable opportunities for local choice. If, as often happened, an independent candidate with his own local connections successfully challenged the sitting Representative, then he could be accommodated with little trouble in the SLPP; in the 1962 election fourteen independents won seats, mostly in Mendeland, and all joined the SLPP a few days later.[46] The situation had altered by 1967, due partly to Albert Margai's attempt to impose his own candidates for the SLPP nomination and partly to the rise of the APC, but even then six independent candidates won seats in the south.

The APC has maintained a stronger central organisation than the SLPP, and a tighter control over the selection of candidates. This was made both possible and necessary by the northern and (to some extent) anti-elite orientations which on the one hand enabled it to appeal to the electorate on grounds independent of the personality and connections of its individual candidates, and on the other hand required it to develop some organisation through which this appeal could be presented.[47] Similar considerations applied to the KPM in Kono and, during its brief existence, to the UDP. These parties almost invariably picked candidates who were natives or long residents of their constituencies and who had some personal resources in them, but they broadened the structure of representation to include people who would never have been elected on personal connections alone.[48] The importance of the APC ticket was most obvious in Freetown, where J. C. O. Hadson-Taylor and J. Barthes Wilson, who came bottom of the poll for the UPP in 1962, won comfortably in the same constituencies for the APC in 1967. The APC's virtually clean sweep of the Northern Province in 1967 also helps to show the strength of the party nomination. In Mendeland, its reputation as a northern party and its inability to gain access to local disputes deprived it in 1967 of all but the tiny proportion of votes produced by northern immigrants; in the 1968–9 by-elections in the south, it therefore followed the SLPP in giving the party symbol to whoever seemed most likely to win among the local independent candidates.

The general election of 1973, in which voting took place in only five constituencies and the APC's nominations were largely decided at the centre, thus marks an important shift from local to central allocation, and a consequent devaluation of the resources available at the periphery. In all but a few cases, the sitting APC MPs were automatically returned; the additional nominations, mostly for newly created seats, went to local men chosen on the basis partly of long service to the party, and partly on adherence to factions within it. In view of the use of Court Presidencies for political patronage, it is not surprising that some of the nominations went to Court Presidents. The SLPP followed its usual custom of picking men with local bases, drawn both from the old SLPP and from UDP sympathisers, but had no chance of getting them elected. A claim made to me by one SLPP organiser that the APC would have won no more than half a dozen seats in the whole country in a fair election doubtless reflects the exaggeration of despair; but the SLPP would certainly have had every chance of winning a majority, and the care taken by the APC to fix the results suggests that – unlike Albert Margai in 1967 – it was under no illusions as to its own unpopularity.

In Liberia, the electoral stage has never in recent times counted for anything, since open opposition to the TWP is impermissible, and recruitment to the Senate and the House of Representatives thus turns entirely on securing the party nomination. This is allocated by a local party caucus at the County level, subject to the President's confirmation (in his role as the party's National Standard Bearer). The party's decision is in practice arrived at by those intricate and informal manoeuvres at both national and local level, in which so much of Liberian politics consists. The process is not entirely closed or unrepresentative, since Liberian politicians acquire considerable expertise in machine politics;[49] when any group of them gather together over a glass of Club or Heineken, the talk is likely to turn to any current nominations, and the merits and prospects of the candidates. What the process does is to place a great deal of emphasis on co-option by and into the group of notables who manage local politics; it equally helps to provide an apprenticeship through which people are inducted into political roles, and to create a fairly realistic set of expectations about an individual's prospects.

Certain conventions have become established. Although both Senators and Representatives are chosen from the County at large rather than for defined constituencies within it, a general principle of territorial balance is maintained. For the Senate, each County is divided roughly in two – Upper and Lower Bong, either side of the Saint Paul River in Montserrado, or the Saint John River in Grand Bassa – and a Senator chosen who has his main links with each. For the

House, the distribution is more complex, but seats are tacitly reserved for certain groups: for 'the tribal people' or the coastal communities, for special sections of each such as the Congos or a group of chiefdoms, and so forth. This in itself helps to weed out those who are not regarded as having any claim on a seat from those who are eligible. For a House seat, a fairly long apprenticeship in local politics is generally needed. For the Senate, which is markedly superior in status, central connections are often required; former top-level Ministers such as Charles B. Sherman of Cape Mount and Harrison Grigsby of Sinoe have retired as Senators to their home counties. In the four hinterland counties, the initial selections comprised one local man and one Senator of coastal origins long resident in the area. Presidential influence is also felt, and Tubman in particular several times insisted on his own nominees despite local opposition.[50] His son is a Senator for Maryland County, and one of the first Lofa County Senators, Willie Belleh, was his former household steward. Presidential support is also useful for any legislator trying to stay in office for more that the conventional two terms.

These methods of selection naturally affect both who become legislators and what they do. The composition of the legislature in each country has been considered in the previous chapter. Apart from the Sierra Leone Representatives' role in selecting and maintaining the party in power at the centre, however, legislators' main functions in both countries are in central–local relations. For the most part, they take these functions seriously, maintaining a house both in their constituency or County headquarters and the capital, and travelling frequently between the two. Apart from a few Liberian Representatives whose role is largely honorific, like Representative Kpangbai of Bong County who died in 1973 at the age of 98, I could not detect any systematic differences in this respect between Liberia and Sierra Leone. There are however considerable differences in the opportunities which legislators have for using their position in the capital in the interests of their constituents. In Sierra Leone, where Ministers and Deputy Ministers are selected from the House of Representatives, they are better able – and are also expected – to use their executive positions for local ends. Cartwright instances the 1962 election, when three-quarters of the SLPP Ministers but only a third of the SLPP backbenchers were returned, as showing the extent to which the Ministers' ability to determine central allocations increases their popularity (or possibly their coercive capability) in their constituencies.[51] Liberian Representatives have no such opportunities, and their capacity to affect allocations depends on their general status in the governing circle; this is where the difference appears between hinterland legislators with few if any central connections, and coastal politicians for whom a seat in the legislature provides a useful base for the exercise of influence.

Influence at the centre in turn affects influence at the periphery, especially in determining the relationships between Representatives and local administrators. In both countries, the comparative stability of the Representative's position gives him some advantage. The reported role of two Americo-Liberian Senators for hinterland Counties in securing the dismissal of their respective Superintendents in 1968 has already been referred to. In Sierra Leone, the rapidly transferred District Officer is in a much weaker position than the Liberian Superintendent, and as a result Representatives take on some of the local political leadership which in Liberia is performed by the Superintendent, for example in publicising government policies and taking the leading role in local self-help projects. Sierra Leone Representatives are also likely to be more closely involved in chieftaincy disputes and other local issues than Liberian ones, because their own political bases are more directly affected.

Finally, both legislators and administrative officials may be by-passed by direct central involvement in the intermediary role, either by local delegations to Freetown or Monrovia, or by ministerial or presidential visits to provincial centres. In Liberia, though important politicians are generally associated with the central government as such rather than with any particular region, they often maintain 'farms' or estates which serve simultaneously as weekend retreats, sources of income, and centres of patronage networks. Tubman's farm at Totota and Tolbert's at Bellefanai, both in Bong County, are the extreme examples of a practice widespread among members of the elite, through which local actors can be brought into contact with central politicians capable of handing out favours. In a country as small as Liberia, these personal contacts may be of appreciable importance in providing individuals with some channel for political demands, and thereby assuring them that the system is not entirely closed to them. Tubman instituted the practice, continued by Tolbert, of paying regular presidential visits to population centres throughout the country in order to go over the heads of local intermediaries by conducting direct transactions with those beneath them. Under Tubman, this was formalised in the Executive Council, an open meeting at which the President would hear and adjudicate complaints against local officials; he sometimes suspended or dismissed the official on the spot, thus providing some check against illegal exactions, gaining popularity and fostering the belief that the President stood for the common people against corrupt officialdom. Tolbert has preferred the surprise visit, suddenly turning up at a County headquarters to inspect, exhort and admonish.

In Sierra Leone, hinterland estates are prevented by the land tenure system, and the Prime Minister or President has not been so well placed to intervene in local politics over the heads of intermediaries within his own government. Milton Margai, certainly, was adept at managing local disputes, but Albert Margai's attempts to exploit the resources to be gleaned from direct central involvement in the local arena were largely unsuccessful.[52] Stevens has visited provincial centres from time to time, to deliver exhortations in favour of national unity and against such practices as diamond smuggling, but has not appeared to be closely involved in political management at the local level.

LINKAGES IN LOCAL POLITICS: HOW, WHO AND WHY?

The previous discussion suggests differences in the linkages through which local politics is related to politics both at the centre and in other local arenas. These can most conveniently be summarised by looking first at the mechanisms which constitute these linkages, then at the types of people who operate and benefit through them, and finally at the functions which they perform, and the problems which they are consequently best and least able to resolve.

The mechanisms for local linkage sharply contrast the single hierarchy of local government in Liberia with the confused pattern of rival linkages in Sierra Leone. This can be connected in turn with the comparative coherence and incoherence of the overall rule structures in the two countries. In Liberia, all roads lead upward to the central source of allocation provided by the President, generally by way of the County-level establishment formed in coastal counties by the party caucus of legislators and senior administrators, and in the hinterland counties above all by the Superintendent. There are some opportunities for finding alternative routes to the centre, by appealing to one established intermediary rather than another, or for cutting out the intervening stages by a direct appeal to the President. But reaching the top -- and, through the same channels, transmitting instructions to the bottom – are what the game is all about. In Sierra Leone, the mechanisms are much more varied. The local administrative leadership is much weaker; party and administrative structures are poorly integrated, except at the chiefdom level in the heyday of the SLPP; and linkages exist not only in order to make contact with the President or Prime Minister, but in order to construct coalitions through opposition parties or rival factions in the governing one. Liberian coastal politicians have every opportunity to collaborate or compete with one another through the core institutions in which they all take part: Tubman's connections with Maryland, Tolbert's with Monserrado and Cape Mount, or Vice-President Greene's with Sinoe, are all brought into politics in this way. Hinterland politicians, by contrast, have little opportunity to collaborate with one another except by way of Monrovia; the traditions of local self-government, which ensure that each County is administered largely by its own natives, at the same time inhibit contacts and exchanges between one County and another. Party mechanisms in Liberia are a means of extending patronage from the centre; in Sierra Leone, ever since the formation of the SLPP, they have been a means of enabling different groups in the hinterland to form alliances with one another, as often as not in opposition to the government in power in Freetown.

Several of the social groups involved in operating these linkages are much the same in the two countries. The Paramount Chief is the main agent at the chiefdom level in each country, though variations in recruitment procedure mean that to some extent different types of people may get the job. Intermediary positions between chiefdom and central levels are most likely to be held in each country by educated hinterlanders. The overall effect of the differences between the two countries is to spread benefits and involvement in Sierra Leone further away from the centre and further down the social scale than in Liberia. Americo-Liberians have acquired an important role in the process, through their hinterland estates, the exercise of their central government offices, and the building of patronage relationships with hinterland clients, which is denied to the Creoles in Sierra Leone. Even within the group of educated hinterlanders, the Liberians have greater incentives to cut themselves off from their own communities, and seek association with the centre, than have Sierra Leoneans. The aspirations of the educated Liberian are perfectly expressed in the distinction between the 'kwi' or 'civilised' and the 'country people' already described. In Sierra Leone, identification with a tribal community has not only lacked the low status which it implies in Liberia, but has also often been a useful source of political support. It has extended political participation by projecting into important positions individuals whose educational qualifications would scarcely have enabled them to get beyond chiefdom level in Liberia: thus, four Cabinet Ministers in Sierra Leone in 1973 had no more than primary education, and three at least of these were men with strong local connections.[53]

Differences in mechanisms and recruitment in turn relate to the fact that the functions of local linkages have been appreciably more varied in Sierra Leone than in Liberia. In Liberia, the function of such linkages is perceived, at least by the administration itself, as being to ensure that the people are godly and quietly governed. A litany of phrases from County Commissioners' reports in the last years of the Tubman administration put the flavour well: 'The people are loyal to the Government and very co-operative in paying their taxes'; 'the political attitude of the tribesmen is normal; the tribal people are loyal to the present Administration'; 'the political activity of the District is calm and pleasing'.[54] Of course, these gratifying sentiments may only partially reflect the Commissioner's view of the situation, and may be downright misleading as a guide to the people's attitudes. But they do accurately reflect the fact that the only available linkages are those through which palavers are settled, taxes collected, beneficent activities in the fields of education, public health and economic development undertaken, and jobs provided for deserving or well-connected individuals. In Sierra Leone, these functions are also carried out, though the funds available for development projects at the local level have steadily declined.[55] But they are overlaid by representative functions which involve the pressing of issues and interests rather than of personal claims and grievances, and which are organised by a class of local politicians of a sort which scarcely appear on the Liberian scene.

The differences come out clearly in the ways in which various kinds of issue are dealt with in the politics of each country. At the lowest level, local politics in both countries draw on factional conflicts, of which the commonest is the chieftaincy dispute. In Liberia, these generally come to the surface only when a new chief is being elected, and though local Commissioners, Representatives or Superintendents may take sides in them to some extent, they are usually settled with a minimum of difficulty at the County level. In Sierra Leone, equivalent conflicts are politicised through involvement in party politics, or in factional divisions within a single party. Complaints against chiefs, which in Liberia are limited to maladministration, extend into the arena of party loyalty, and may be activated whenever a change of national government gives a chief's opponents cause to hope that their allegations against him will be well received. Hence the Sierra Leone system intensifies this kind of conflict while the Liberian one plays it down; the Sierra Leonean system may be more open and representative, but it pays a price in chiefdom-level fragmentation and uncertainty.

A second level of conflict is concerned with competition for benefits, particularly for government financial allocations. In Liberia, this is largely a matter for individual claimants, especially those seeking jobs. There is no mechanism by which groups of people may be organised to demand benefits for their County or their social or economic grouping; rather, the Superintendent or a legislator might take it on himself to seek a favourable ruling from the President on the location of a new road, or the alignment of a County boundary. In Sierra Leone, these are matters for more public politics: the leading politicians made their way into politics as spokesmen for various ethnic, regional or economic interests, and still to some extent represent them, even though the decline of the competitive party system has removed the main control which the rank and file had over their leaders.

A third level of conflict is concerned with the selection of, and representation in, the government itself. Here the Liberian system has very little to offer. The government is an external source of exaction and allocation over which individuals outside the magic circle have no control. Sierra Leone for a time presented the rare spectacle of a government which countryside votes had elected (whatever the limitations under which that choice was expressed), and which they could in turn remove. That failed to last, but the sense of representation in government, through Ministers from one's own tribe or District, not totally unsusceptible to local pressure, is still very much greater than in Liberia.

CHAPTER 7

ASPECTS OF POLITICAL ECONOMY

POLITICAL AND ECONOMIC STRUCTURES

An economy is the purest form of political system. Like other political systems, but in a particularly clear way, it provides a structure within which actors combine and compete with one another in pursuit of prizes. It incorporates a diverse collection of resources which may be useful in gaining these prizes, and a rule structure which sets the terms of exchange between the resources. It combines, too, the productive activities necessary for the maintenance of the society with the extractive, distributive and often coercive ones through which benefits are allocated, and through which those in advantaged positions generally seek to protect the rules which favour their own access to prizes. It is important to note that these rules consist not only in economic patterns of production and exchange, but equally in any kind of social, political or coercive pressure through which actors can extract a favourable share of the available allocations for themselves. The economy is thus not simply a source of influence on 'the political system': it *is* a political system, in which resources and relationships are combined, clarified and to some extent rendered measurable by their common concern with the prizes implicit in wealth.

Characteristically, actors have a common interest in the maintenance and growth of the economic processes through which wealth is created, but conflicting interests in the allocation of the wealth itself. Thus they seek to outmanoeuvre one another to improve their own allocations without upsetting the overall productive apparatus on which all rely. This manoeuvring may itself involve a temporary threat to the productive apparatus in order to improve a group's bargaining position, most obviously in the case of a strike. More basic upsets are likely when one group feels that it can totally squeeze out another without destroying the productive apparatus, or when a disadvantaged group feels its own allocations to be so poor that it has nothing much to lose by seeking to destroy this apparatus or parts of it altogether. Political economy is the combination of conflict, bargaining and co-operation through which the competition for allocations takes place.

In Sierra Leone and Liberia, as in most developing countries, the structure of competition is set by the implicit imbalances between the nature and distribution of government power and those of economic production. Government power is determined by the boundaries of the state. Within those boundaries, the governments of Sierra Leone and Liberia are independent not simply in some formal constitutional sense, but through their control of force and an administrative apparatus, and their ability to make rules to which other actors must conform. The theoretical threat of losing this independence through foreign invasion is not one of which they need in practice take much account. Economic production, on the other hand, is very heavily geared to flows across state boundaries, in particular of minerals and agricultural produce to the industrialised economies, and of manufactures (but also food) from them. The domestic economies of Liberia and Sierra Leone are so closely enmeshed with the international market that withdrawal from it is inconceivable. Almost every sector of the economy apart from subsistence agriculture depends directly or indirectly on foreign trade and the revenues which it provides; even subsistence agriculture can scarcely be excluded, since it is supplemented and sustained by growing cash crops for export, and by the proceeds of casual labour in mining or the towns.

The external penetration of the domestic economy makes itself felt in several ways. One of them is to restrict appreciably the governments' freedom of action in economic management. The currency provides an illustration. Liberia uses the American dollar as currency, and standard issue US notes circulate with Liberian coins. A fair case can be made that this is in Liberia's interest, in that confidence in the currency and freedom from the inflation caused by runaway note issues more than make up for the impossibility of having an independent monetary policy; Guinea tends to be held up as the awful warning. Sierra Leone has its own currency, the Leone, but this is pegged to sterling and has to be kept convertible so as to minimise the smuggling of diamonds (especially, of course, into Liberia in exchange for US dollars) which would otherwise occur. Hence the effective economic constraints on Sierra Leone's currency are much the same as those on Liberia's, even though the symbolic dependence is not so obvious. The constraints on the governments of small underdeveloped countries produced by fluctuating primary produce prices, debt servicing, the difficulty of controlling multinational corporations, and so forth, are sufficiently well known to need no further emphasis.[1]

Another political consequence of external penetration is the presence of foreigners and the resentment which this arouses, either through their wealth or through the belief that they deny jobs and opportunities to indigenous producers. Much of the most overt anti-foreign activity has been directed against Africans from nearby states, including demonstrations against Guinean Foulahs in Sierra Leone in 1969, and the attacks on the Ibo quarter in Monrovia which followed a murder committed by an Ibo in the same year. But there have also been strikes against foreign corporations such as Firestone in Liberia and the big foreign stores in Freetown; and though open hostility to the Lebanese has been astonishingly slight, there is no question about their general unpopularity.[2]

Finally, the government itself depends heavily on economic relations with the outside world for its own income.[3] In Sierra Leone, anything between 67% and

and 76% of estimated revenues between 1968 and 1974 were directly attributable to foreign trade and the operations of foreign companies. In Liberia, the proportion dropped steadily from 86.4% in 1960 to 78.6% in 1966, and then on down to 61.3% in 1972, though these, it must be emphasised, are minimum figures, and take no account of domestically raised revenue indirectly attributable to foreign trade, such as income taxes on expatriate employees, or hut taxes paid by the sale of exported cash crops. Essentially then, the governments of both countries keep themselves going by taxing the movement of goods across their frontiers.

But this dependence is not entirely a one-way process. The governmental powers derived from national sovereignty and control of the state apparatus are to some extent autonomous. Whatever the government's ultimate dependence on the international economy, immediate threats to its position generally come from dissatisfied groups within the domestic society. The impact of the international economy itself creates resentments which may lead the government to take action against its most visible local representatives. Government can use its regulatory powers to extract payments from foreign entrepreneurs, who themselves depend on government tolerance for their presence in the country. Thus domestic politicians can act as brokers between domestic society and international economy, extracting resources from both sides and managing the exchanges between them so as to maintain and strengthen their own position. Alternatively if they are unskilful, if the gap between the requirements of the international economy and those of domestic political support is too great to be bridged, or if the financial resources extracted are too small to support the government apparatus, then the governing groups may find themselves squeezed out of their brokerage role and consequently lose power.

Thus the resources involved in politico-economic competition derive partly from control over various forms of productive activity, and partly from opportunities for regulation and coercion. Different combinations of these resources help to define the principal groups of competing actors. Three main ones may usefully be distinguished, though the boundaries between them are not always clear, and each may be further divided into sections which compete with one another.

The first group are the foreign producers. They are of foreign origin (though individuals may acquire local citizenship), and manage most of the transactions between the domestic economy and the outside world, as well as having, inevitably, considerable influence in the domestic economy itself. The most important resource at their disposal is their management of, or access to, the multinational organisation on which a penetrated import–export oriented economy depends. This in turn leads them to possess, in varying degrees, special skills in running complex organisations and advanced technological processes, and the ability to raise large amounts of capital. At the top of the range, this group most obviously includes the big corporations responsible for extracting natural resources in minerals and agriculture. In Sierra Leone, the most important are Sierra Leone Selection Trust (SLST) in diamond mining and Sierra Leone Development Company (Delco) in iron ore, both of which are subsidiaries of British companies; though the Sierra Leone government took a 51% stake in the diamond mining operation in 1971, SLST remains responsible for running it. In Liberia, they include the main iron ore companies, LAMCO and Bong Mining Company, with American, Swedish, German and Canadian participation, and the American rubber plantations of Firestone and B. F. Goodrich. The manufacturing sector, concentrated in Freetown and Monrovia, is also heavily foreign run. The remaining foreign producers are mostly concerned with trade. The large foreign banks are mostly British in Sierra Leone and American in Liberia, and the leading import–export houses in both countries are mostly British and European. The next layer comprises wholesalers and retailers, who include some Greeks and Indians, but are mostly Syrian and Lebanese. And finally, there are the West African petty traders, fishermen, taxi-drivers and so forth, who are distinguished from indigenous Sierra Leoneans and Liberians not so much by their economic functions as by their alienness and consequently by their lack of influence on government. The great bargaining weakness of the whole foreign producer group is indeed the fact that they are foreigners, which denies them a role in government and is only very partially offset by such diplomatic influence as their home governments can exert.

The second group, the indigenous producers, include the peasantry and producers of agricultural cash crops; the local labour employed by foreign companies in rubber-tapping, iron-ore mining, trading and manufacturing; the indigenous petty traders, with a few rather larger entrepreneurs; and, at least in Sierra Leone, the ever hopeful hordes of illicit diamond miners. Their economic bargaining power does not equal that of the foreign producers, since they do not have the same access to international transactions, and their influence is generally limited to those stages of production and distribution which take place within the country: the bargaining power of the most influential of them, the diamond miners, is indeed due in large measure to their ability to smuggle their product abroad. Nor are many of them in much position to take strike action, though every now and then a successful strike can improve the position of those in unionised labour. The other resources available to them depend largely on their access to government, through elections, riots, or some other pressure which leads government to feel that it needs to take their interests into account; indeed a strike may often be not so much an imposition of economic bargaining power, as an implicit appeal to government to support indigenous workers against a foreign corporation.

Some indigenous producers come into a category of their own, precisely because this access to government can be turned, through their own involvement in politics, into a regular source of economic opportunity. The most obvious field for this is in government contracting, but the principle can be extended to any area of the economy where political influence can be used to provide advantages in economic competition. This is especially clear in Liberia, where most leading politicians combine government office with private opportunities for making money. This phenomenon will be examined in the next section.

The third group, then, is the government itself, and the individuals and sectional organisations who act through it. Its characteristic resource is the coercive power of the state, and its first concern is to extract from the economy the means which it needs to maintain itself; this is true of any governmental organisation, but it has become especially important with the superimposition of an ever-expanding structure of government jobs on a narrow economic base. At the same time, governments engage in a number of productive activities, sometimes with monopoly powers and sometimes in the open market. Produce marketing boards combine both functions, by marketing crops and at the same time creaming off a profit for government use. Governments equally produce services such as education and health, and encourage production by other groups through concessions, development plans, and so forth.

All of these groups have some interest in creating sources of wealth from which they may benefit, but all of them likewise are competing for the resulting allocations and any one of them may seek to improve its pay-off by combining with another against the third. The government and a foreign business may combine to defeat a strike; the government may ally itself with indigenous producers in order to limit the opportunities open to foreign traders; or – as most obviously with illicit diamond-mining in Sierra Leone – indigenous producers and foreigners with access to world markets may combine in order to evade the exactions imposed by government. Political comparison is then concerned with the terms on which the resulting pattern of competition and co-operation takes place, the relationships which it involves between groups, and the distribution of benefits which results. Similarities and differences between Liberia and Sierra Leone may then be related to the economic situation of the two countries, and the aspects of their political structure already outlined.

GOVERNMENT, FOREIGN AND INDIGENOUS PRODUCERS

Modern economic growth in both Liberia and Sierra Leone has been brought about by the introduction of foreign producers, and by a close alliance between them and government. This has been most marked in Liberia. The Firestone agreement of 1926 provided Liberia with what remained for some twenty-five years almost its only source of foreign exchange, and led to the use of government powers to provide an adequate supply of effectively forced labour to the Firestone plantations. It had the great disadvantage, from the government's viewpoint, of making it over dependent on a single foreign company. One of the successful aims of Tubman's Open Door Policy, and the use of the US dollar as a currency, was to reduce this dependence by bringing in a variety of other concessions, in iron ore mining, logging, fruit growing, and some manufacturing enterprises.[4] In the process, the relationship with foreign producers as a whole was strengthened. In Sierra Leone, a similar though less spectacular programme took place under the colonial government, especially with the advent of SLST and Delco during the 1930s. No new enterprises on the same scale made their appearance during the subsequent forty years, but the independent government continued to favour foreign investment, and kept in force the Development Ordinance of 1960 which allowed tax holidays and government loans for new industries; most of the businesses which took advantage of these concessions would probably have come to Sierra Leone even without them.[5]

This economic relationship with foreign corporations leads easily to the assumption that these corporations must play a large part in government. In fact, there is little evidence to suggest that they do, and no great reason to suppose it. The government and the corporations have a common interest in maintaining a source of wealth from which both profit, and in the normal course of events there is no reason for either to disrupt it. Problems in the relationship arise, not from corporation involvement in the affairs of government, but rather from government involvement in those of the corporation, either on behalf of dissatisfied indigenous producers, or to increase the share of the total pay off which accrues to government. When this happens, the options at the corporation's disposal are limited. The easiest, and generally the most effective, is to make some concession to government pressure, and to retreat into arguments based on economic niceties, which may be true or false but which in any case the government will be unable to follow. It is common, especially in Liberia, for members of the government – acting for example through their private legal practices – to receive retainers from corporations, though this may be regarded more as a means by which elite members extort money from the corporations, than as one by which the corporations subvert government. The only cases of more direct attempts to intervene in national politics which I have come across are reported gifts by foreign businessmen, including SLST, to the SLPP in the 1962 and 1967 elections, but these equally were extortions as much as they were bribes.[6]

The governments in both countries have for their part made no attempt to reshape relationships in any very drastic way and have taken only a very limited role in economic management. State corporations are almost non-existent in the laissez-faire Liberian economy, and are few in Sierra Leone: they include the Diamond Mining Corporation, managed by SLST, the Forest Industries Corporation at Kenema, and public utilities such as Sierra Leone Airways and the Produce Marketing Board. Except for a brief burst of contractor finance projects under Albert Margai, most of them unsuccessful, the state has not sought to act as an entrepreneur in competition with the private sector.[7] Both countries have Ministries of Planning, but in both, their efforts have scarcely gone beyond indicative planning with slight implications for government budgeting and very little impact beyond it.[8] The two main areas in which governments have attempted to reshape the economy have been the partial nationalisation of SLST in Sierra Leone, and the indigenisation of trade in both countries; these are considered in later sections.

Within this framework of continuity, there have been some changes in emphasis in economic policy in both countries, all corresponding closely to the general political orientations of the respective regimes. In Liberia, though government spokesmen have strenuously denied any change in the principles of the open door policy, the Tolbert administration has increasingly emphasised the need for Liberians to gain a larger share of the proceeds, and has criticised some foreign companies, especially Firestone.[9] This shift can be related not only to Tolbert's need to generate popular support and distinguish his government from his predecessor's, but equally to the need to find jobs and revenues to meet the increasing demands on government once foreign investment starts to fall off. In Sierra Leone, the combination of conservatism and local brokerage in Milton Margai's government was perfectly reflected in an economic policy which introduced no overall development scheme, but rather produced piecemeal projects in response to pressures from local politicians.[10] This was arguably more effective than Albert Margai's policy, which in keeping with other aspects of his government was more centralised and more grandiose than his brother's, and resulted in a number of white-elephant projects of which the best known was the Lumley Beach Hotel. It is also symptomatic that Milton's approach diffused opportunities for corruption through the hinterland chiefly elite, notably through such devices as the Building Materials Scheme,[11] while Albert's resulted in more obvious corruption by central government ministers.[12] The NRC, true to its belief in good government, invited help from the International Monetary Fund, whose resident representative in Freetown became one of its most influential advisors.[13] The Stevens government has adopted a piecemeal approach, most similar to Milton Margai's, but reflecting a rather different balance of forces and the greater influence of the centre. Economic policy and political structure have thus been closely related.

Nowhere is this clearer than in the connections between political office and economic opportunity within the Liberian government. One of the most distinctive features of the political economy of Liberia is the combination of government office with private economic enterprise. The great majority of Liberian officials, from ministers down to rural petty functionaries, possess in addition to their government jobs some private source of income. At the rural level, this is usually a rice farm, or else possibly a couple of taxis or a small cocoa or rubber plantation. As one rises within the government hierarchy, so also does one's scale of business. The largest and best known of all Liberian businesses is the Mesurado group, founded by the President's late brother and Minister of Finance, Stephen Tolbert, which has expanded from the original Mesurado Fishing Company to include the Swiss-African Trading Company, an import–export business handling the franchises for British Leyland cars and Carrier airconditioning, and several other enterprises. One common form of enterprise is a law firm, such as the C. Cecil Dennis Law Firm managed by the Minister of Foreign Affairs, or the big Henries Law Firm owned by the Speaker of the House of Representatives. These provide opportunities for contacts both with other members of the governing elite – Cecil Dennis manages the Mesurado brief – and with foreign corporations. Other officials may be in the transport business, as with the prominent YES bus and taxi company owned by Police chief Tommy Bernard, or they may own plantations or timber concessions in the interior. Many businesses, too, are directly linked with government through public works contracting or the lease to government of privately owned buildings.

These connections between private business and public office are not nearly so prominent in Sierra Leone. The import–export business in goods such as cars and airconditioners is largely in the hands of long-established foreign firms, though some of the newer franchises – for Japanese cars, for instance – are controlled by Lebanese. The land tenure system inhibits the acquisition of large plantations in the hinterland by Freetown-based politicians, though a few hinterland politicians, such as A. G. Sembu-Forna, former Minister of Agriculture, have started private agricultural development schemes in their home areas. Other inhibiting factors are the more precarious position of the governing elites, and the less prominent political position of Creoles, who share with Americo-Liberians a disproportionate amount of their country's stock of professional skills, but do not have the same opportunities for combining them with political office.

Further relationships between political structure and economic bargaining are most easily examined by looking at the three main sectors of the economy in turn.

TRADE

Trade in both Liberia and Sierra Leone has been almost entirely in foreign hands, except at the lowest level of petty hawking, and in a few areas susceptible to government control such as produce-marketing in Sierra Leone and government contracting in Liberia. The Cox-George Commission in Sierra Leone found that in 1955 no more than 2.1% of imports and 1.5% of exports were handled by African concerns, which also owned only 11.8% of registered retail stores;[14] since even this percentage must include many Guineans as well as Nigerians and Ghanaians, the total for Sierra Leoneans must be even smaller. Apart from the politicians' businesses already referred to, there is no reason to suppose that the figures for Liberia would be any greater. Since trading does not obviously require the capital, technological expertise, or large-scale organisation needed for mining or manufacturing, it is an obvious target for attempts by government to increase indigenous participation in the economy. The politics of trade has therefore largely been concerned with the restrictions to be placed on foreigners, and the consequent benefits to be gained by indigenous groups. Indigenous consumers, who would bear most of the consequences in price or supply of any decline in the overall efficiency of distributive networks, have scarcely been a group to be reckoned with.

Indigenous petty traders are better organised in Sierra Leone than in Liberia, and have had greater opportunities for presenting their case to government, so that it is scarcely surprising that the earliest steps towards indigenisation were taken there. Foreigners were prohibited from participating in the rice trade in 1962, and the Albert Margai government in 1965 passed an act restricting foreign involvement in the building materials, transport and bakery trades, and leaving wide ministerial discretion for excluding them from other areas.[15] This law was revoked by the NRC, but was restored and extended by the APC government in 1969.[16] The 1969 Act was accompanied by a demand from the Sierra Leone Petty Traders Association that all Nigerian, Ghanaian, Gambian and other African traders should be asked to leave, as well as by attacks on Guinean Foulahs who were generally regarded as SLPP supporters.[17] The Sierra Leone Labour Congress, on the other hand, called on the government to exclude the larger foreign firms from the act so as to safeguard its members' jobs.[18] The act can thus largely be seen as a reaction by the government to the demands of its grassroots supporters, but despite emollient speeches and occasional expulsions not much has been done to implement it. There is general agreement that the number of Guineans trading in Sierra Leone increased markedly in the five years after 1969, and the government's close relations with – and for a period military dependence on – Guinea, limited the amount it could do.[19] The shift in the government's own resource base thus affected the opportunities open to foreign and indigenous petty traders.

In Liberia, where the Guinean presence is just as marked, petty traders have never had the entrée to government, and no steps were taken to reserve areas of trade to Liberians until the 1970s. As part of his attempt after taking over the Presidency to generate new political resources, Tolbert announced that some fields, especially in transport, were to be reserved to Liberians. The immediate effect of this has been not so much to provide opportunities for lower paid Liberians as to clear the way for enterprises operated by members of the elite.[20] The Director of the National Police Force, the Minister of Planning, and the former Commissioner of Internal Revenue in 1973 all ran flourishing taxi businesses, and other ministers were taking advantage of the indigenisation measures to set themselves up in the petrol-station trade. Indigenisation, both in Liberia and Sierra Leone, has led to well-placed politicians nominally taking over Lebanese businesses, and leaving the original owners to continue in management while the sleeping partner prevents government interference and participates in the profits. Other exactions are more blatant: the Liberian government ruled in 1967 that Lebanese merchants should deposit $10,000 with it as caution money against 'mercantile malpractices';[21] and in Sierra Leone, especially in the diamond dealing area, Lebanese may find themselves having to pay substantial sums to politicians in order to stay in business.[22]

The alien status of the Lebanese has been reinforced by the indigenous government. In Liberia, where citizenship of the Republic has from its foundation been reserved to persons of Negro African descent, they have automatically been excluded from formal political participation.[23] In Sierra Leone, where all British subjects and British protected persons, regardless of race, became entitled to citizenship at independence, more explicit measures were needed to keep them out. These were prompted by the 1962 general election, when several SLPP leaders evidently felt that wealthy Lebanese might successfully stand against them.[24] The resulting Sierra Leone Nationality and Citizenship Act, with two associated constitutional amendments, provided that only those whose father and father's father were of Negro African origin could be citizens by birth; other persons could only become naturalised citizens at the discretion of the appropriate Minister, could have their citizenship revoked at any time, and could not stand for the House of Representatives.[25] This was replaced in 1973 by a second act which eased the position of the children of foreign fathers and Sierra Leonean mothers, but required citizens naturalised under the previous act to reapply.[26] So far, there has been no proposal in either country to expel the Lebanese, and a Liberian Minister of Information who appeared to be threatening them with the fate meted out by General Amin to the Uganda Asians was instantly dismissed;[27] but denied any possibility of integration, their position in both countries is perennially insecure.[28]

There are some fields in which indigenisation results in the transfer to indigenous hands of functions which would otherwise be performed by foreigners. The Mesurado Fishing Corporation owned by the late Finance Minister Stephen Tolbert supplies a staple item in the Liberian diet which would otherwise have to be imported. The Swiss-African Trading Corporation, also owned by Stephen Tolbert, and the Technico-Auriole Company of former Secretary of State Rocheforte Weeks carry out export–import business which in Sierra Leone is still in the hands of metropolitan companies such as UAC and CFAO. The restriction of produce-buying to Liberians since 1972 – a step not yet paralleled in Sierra Leone – has diminished countryside dependence on the Lebanese, and encouraged the formation of marketing co-operatives.[29] For most purposes though, indigenisation in both countries, though most blatantly in Liberia, is a means by which those in political power gain access to economic rewards.

MINING

The extraction of minerals, especially iron ore and diamonds, accounts for an overwhelming percentage of the exports, and a substantial proportion of gross national product and government revenues, in both countries.[30] Iron ore mining requires a very high initial capital investment and vertically integrated mining, processing and marketing arrangements, and is entirely in the hands of large foreign companies or consortia. Diamond mining does not so obviously need the capital and organisation which only a large corporation can provide, though international marketing is closely integrated by the De Beers/Diamond Corporation group and its numerous offshoots. The politics of mining are therefore largely concerned with attempts by government to extract maximum payments from foreign concessionaires; with attempts to increase payments by the concessionaires to local factors of production in the form of pay, employment, and use of local goods and services; and with the three-cornered fight between government, foreign and indigenous producers over the wealth extracted from the Sierra Leonean diamond fields.

The first two of these areas are ones in which the similarities in the bargaining situation of the governments of two small African states dealing with multinational companies are likely to outweigh differences due to domestic political structure. The similarities are reinforced by the basically favourable attitude of both governments towards foreign investment, despite some rhetorical radicalism by the Albert Margai and Stevens governments in Sierra Leone. Though both governments are anxious to gain as much as possible from the mining companies, neither is prepared to squeeze them so hard as to risk them leaving altogether. As Stevens so aptly put it; 'we have no intention of killing the goose that lays the golden eggs'.[31] As against this, the Liberian government's efforts to expand total production through the open door policy may be expected to have led it to accept a lower unit return than in Sierra Leone.

The two countries are most directly comparable in the iron-ore field, though even here, differences in the quality of ore, royalty or profit-sharing arrangements, and other details of the concession agreements make precise comparison almost impossible. The most one can do is see whether there are any marked differences in the total amounts which the governments are able to extract. Delco, in Sierra Leone, mines ore which is about 40% pure, and is concentrated to 63–4% pure, about 2,500,000 tons of concentrate being exported each year. Until 1972, it made direct payments to the Sierra Leone government of Le0.02 royalty on each ton of concentrate and a 50% income tax on profits, though the company made a loss in both 1971 and 1972. Following the government's abanment of a proposal to take a 51% controlling interest in Delco, a new agreement was negotiated in 1973, replacing that which had been in effect unaltered since 1956.[32] This raised royalties to Le0.06 per ton, and income tax to 60%, as well as raising the rent payable on the Marampa concessions to Le20,000 per annum. This rent, payable to the Chiefdom authorities, has no equivalent in Liberia, and indicates the greater bargaining power of the local level in Sierra Leone. To these direct payments must be added customs duties which, on Delco's estimate, come to some Le400,000 per annum,[33] leaving a total payment to central government in a profitless year of about Le550,000 or Le0.22 ($0.26) per ton.

The Liberian concession most directly comparable to Delco is the Bong

Mining Company (BMC), which is run by a German consortium under the title of Deutsch-Liberian Mining Company (Delimco), which also mines ore at 40% pure and concentrates it to 65%. The Liberian government receives 50% of profits *or* a royalty of $0.25 per ton, whichever is higher. As against this, BMC like other concessions has received blanket duty-free privileges, which not only deprive the government of income, but encourage the companies to import goods rather than using local supplies. In 1972, for example, the import duties of $2,018,500 foregone by the government on BMC's non-capital imports were appreciably greater than the $1,668,500 received through profit-sharing. Renegotiation of the concession in 1973 resulted in BMC agreeing to make a token payment in lieu of duty of $150,000, and to make increased use of local supplies.[34] On 1972 production figures of 7,690,000 tons, this would provide a total minimum payment to government of $0.27 per ton, with more in profitable years.

So far as it is possible to calculate, then, the receipts to the two governments have been roughly the same, though had Delco been run as profitably as BMC, the Sierra Leone government would have done appreciably better. The Liberian government's receipts from the high grade iron ore mined by Lamco in Nimba County, at $0.60–0.70 per ton, are much higher than those from either Delco or BMC.[35] The available figures are inadequate to compare returns to local factors of production, though one report puts them at about 27% for the Liberian iron ore industry as a whole.[36] Wages for unskilled workers in the two countries are also similar; in 1961, the latest year for which I can find comparable figures, they were Le0.60 ($0.84) a day at Delco, against $0.10 an hour (say $0.80 a day) at the Bomi Hills mine in Liberia, plus perks including food.[37]

Detailed supervision by government in both countries is made almost impossible by the companies' financial arrangements and especially the opportunities for transfers within the company. Delco and BMC, for example, have raised capital from associated companies, on which interest is paid, and have consultancy agreements with their parent organisations. BMC sells most of its ore to the German steel companies which own it, creating opportunities for transferring profits through internal pricing mechanisms, though Delco sells its ore on the open market, much of it to Japan. These are the standard problems in dealing with international companies.

Some of the same problems arise in the Sierra Leone diamond mining industry, especially through the dominant position of the international diamond market held by the Diamond Corporation group (DiCor). DiCor buys half of the output of the main Sierra Leone producer, SLST/Diminco, it runs the Government Diamond Office which buys privately mined diamonds (many of them illegally extracted from the Diminco reserves), and it operates buying agencies in Liberia for diamonds smuggled out of Sierra Leone.[38] Thus the same diamond may be sold to the same corporation in any of three different ways. DiCor's interest in maintaining the world price of diamonds coincides with that of the producing countries, and by preventing wide fluctuations it has benefited local producers. At the same time, the pervasiveness of its operations prevents the producer from gaining any fully independent valuation of the product, and prevents the Sierra Leone government from ensuring that it gains the maximum benefit from the industry. In March 1974, the Sierra Leone government licensed five new diamond-buying agencies to compete with DiCor, but these still only account for a small share of the trade.[39]

In other respects, however, the political implications of diamond mining are very different from those of iron ore. Iron ore is valuable only in bulk, and its extraction requires heavy capital investment and is easily controlled. A diamond the size of a fingernail may be worth thousands of dollars; it can be picked up by anyone, smuggled with ease, and readily exchanged for cash. As a result, illegal mining takes place on a large scale, and employs not only Sierra Leoneans but powerful foremen from other West African countries (especially, it is said, the Gambia), and licensed diamond dealers most of whom are Lebanese. The resources generated by their operations (in cash, but also in violence) are enough to buy off or subvert attempts at control, and to create powerful interests for their continuation. The triangular competition for the proceeds of diamond mining between DiCor and SLST, private operators, and the Sierra Leone government gives rise to a wealth of rumours – of bribery, smuggling, witchcraft, and political malpractice – amongst which the truth is impossible to establish.

The SLST's position has fairly clearly deteriorated. Until 1956, it possessed – though it was unable to enforce – a legal monopoly over diamond mining. In that year the monopoly was ended, partly because of political pressures arising from increased representation, but equally because smuggling led to a loss of revenues which no government could afford to ignore. Alluvial miners and diamond dealers were licensed to operate privately and a Government Diamond Office was set up to buy stones from them on a 'no questions asked' basis. This intensified the pressures on the SLST mining areas, especially as the government could scarcely give SLST the physical protection which it demanded for its leases, without alienating local electoral support. Though SLST has continued to operate the mines since the 51% takeover in 1971, it is subject to government pressures for indigenisation and other management changes, and over the rate of depletion of reserves.

The government itself is in a trickier position. It gains much of its income from official diamond mining through SLST/Diminco, and thus has an interest in defending Diminco's concession area against invasion by illicit miners. Illicit and semi-illicit operations, on the other hand, are a source both of wealth and of political support. On the whole, the SLPP has tended to favour the SLST and the diamond areas chiefs, while the APC with its local allies, the KPM and DPC, has been the party of the illicit miners, though shifts between government and opposition have affected their positions. In the 1962 elections, DiCor felt it worthwhile to give Le50,000, and SLST a further Le40,000, to the SLPP.[40] Both parties have had links with leading Lebanese diamond dealers. Despite periodical crackdowns on foreigners in the diamond areas, and exhortations against illicit mining, the APC government since 1968 has done little to prevent it, and collusion between diamond dealers and ministers is readily assumed.

The Liberian diamond industry is heavily parasitic on Sierra Leone, since only a few low quality diamonds are mined in the country, and it gains most of its produce from operating buying agencies for high quality Sierra Leonean gem stones smuggled across the border. A desire to combine this profitable trade with good relations with their neighbour leads the Liberians to enter diamond exports in their trade figures at about a fifth of their actual value.[41] Joint pronouncements on preventing smuggling are a staple part of Liberian–Sierra Leone diplomatic exchanges. From the standpoint of domestic Liberian politics, however, the trade has no special importance.

AGRICULTURE

Whereas the politics of mining is largely concerned with relations between government and foreign producers, that of agriculture is concerned largely with relations between government and indigenous producers. There are exceptions in each category: the big rubber plantations in Liberia involve foreign companies, just as the diamond industry in Sierra Leone has to take account of indigenous miners. But the overall patterns are different, and in agriculture give greater scope for variations which can be traced back to, and have an effect on, the domestic political system. The two main political issues involved in agriculture are, firstly, the question of access to agricultural resources, especially land and labour; and secondly the question of payments to, and extraction from, the agricultural sector, through taxation, produce marketing arrangements, and the incomes of agricultural wage earners.

The most obvious differences are in access to land, and relate directly to the colonisation of the Liberian interior under the control of the coastal settlers, as against the alliance between the colonial government and indigenous peoples which largely excluded the Creoles from access to the hinterland in Sierra Leone. All land in Liberia is initially owned by the state, but may be alienated by it into fee simple private ownership. The main exceptions to this rule are the government forest reserves, and the tribal reserve lands set aside for the subsistence of communities in the hinterland. The remaining land may be sold by the state, at a flat rate currently of $30 an acre for urban land and $0.50 an acre for other land.[42] These prices are themselves an indication that there is no land shortage in Liberia, except in areas such as Monrovia where all available government land has long ago been sold. In order to buy land, it is first essential to get a Tribal Certificate, granting the consent of the local tribal authorities, including the Paramount Chief, Clan Chief and elders; for this a payment is made, originally a token in kind, but now more often in cash. The grant has then to be confirmed by the President and registered with the courts.

This procedure makes it possible for any Liberian to buy land, regardless of his place or community of origin, and a great many Americo-Liberians and educated hinterlanders, as well as chiefdom authorities, have taken advantage of it to acquire farms or plantations in the interior. Bong/Kpai Chiefdom, for example, contains rubber, cocoa and oil-palm plantations owned by five Americo-Liberians (including an ex-Ambassador, a Major in the Army, a former Director of Police, and a Representative), as well as a Mandingo trader, a former County Superintendent, and the current Paramount Chief.[43] Foreigners may not own land, but may lease it from private owners or (especially with the larger concessions) from the government. Thus, land-holding in Liberia encourages investment in agriculture, and provides opportunities for productive investment within the country, though at the same time these opportunities go mostly to those members of the coastal and hinterland elites who have the capital and connections to exploit them.

Since land is for the most part in plentiful supply, this system does not give rise to intolerable abuse, and it is said that local people generally welcome new plantations for the money-earning opportunities which they provide. The main complaints have come from the exaction of labour rather than of land.[44] The use of forced labour was at the root of the League of Nations crisis in 1930,[45] and as a result of agricultural development in the hinterland and a continued shortage of labour, some of the same problems have remained. The Northwestern survey discusses cases of involuntary or semi-voluntary recruitment through the Department of Interior or the chiefs in the early 1960s,[46] and one of the reasons given me for wanting to become chief in 1973 was the advantage it provided in getting labour for one's farms.

In Sierra Leone, by contrast, fee simple land tenure exists only in the Freetown Peninsula. Elsewhere, formal ownership is vested in the Tribal Authorities of each Paramount Chiefdom, who may allocate but not alienate it.[47] For natives of the chiefdom, holding customary land rights within it, tenure is in practice secure. Strangers – anyone from outside the chiefdom – may lease land, but it is commonly believed that they will be allowed to enjoy it in peace only so long as it is not worth anything; attempts to improve the land, by planting valuable tree crops for instance, will result in claims being made on it, in which the stranger will be at a disadvantage.[48] This especially affects the Creoles, who have no native chiefdom, and at the same time have a disproportionate amount of the capital available for investment, and their complaints at the system have been long and loud; the fact that hinterlanders can buy them out of their own home territory in Freetown adds further injury. Some wealthy hinterlanders have established large farms in their home chiefdoms, but for the most part there is less investment than in Liberian agriculture, and cash-crop farming is carried out by smallholders rather than large estates.

These different means of production make it impossible to compare returns to agricultural workers between the two countries. Presumably a Sierra Leonean smallholder will do better than a Liberian plantation employee – though there are plenty of smallholders in Liberia, too. However, wage rates at the Firestone rubber plantation – the largest single employer of agricultural labour – show a marked increase, from $0.25 a day for an unskilled rubber tapper in 1950, to $0.45 in 1962, $0.64 in 1963, and $1.50 in 1969.[49] Wages on privately owned plantations have consistently been less than on the big foreign ones, since their owners have greater access to semi-voluntary labour and are not so vulnerable to political pressures. In July 1973, President Tolbert announced an increase in the minimum agricultural wage from $0.08 to $0.12½ per hour,[50] but there is no saying how many workers receive it.

The other main issue in agricultural politics is the amount which farmers receive for their crops or – which comes to the same thing – the rake-off which the government makes between buying cash crops from their producers and selling them on the world market. In both countries, produce-marketing is carried out by a government monopoly which fixes the prices which its agents should pay the producer. The Liberian Produce Marketing Corporation (LPMC) is managed by the Danish Ost Asiatiske Compagnie (OAC) under a fifty-fifty ownership and profit-sharing agreement with the government, whereas the Sierra Leone Produce Marketing Board (SLPMB) is a wholly governmental operation, and hence more open to political manipulation. There are also differences in management policy, in that the LPMC's producer prices are strongly geared to the world market price, allowing only a small provision for price stabilisation; the SLPMB, on the other hand, reckons to keep its producer prices more steady, making substantial profits during periods of high world prices, and subsidising producers during low ones. The profits, at any rate, are a reality. In the fifteen years between 1949 and 1963, the Board netted Le1,147,600 in cocoa operations alone, as well as providing the government with Le2,075,600 in cocoa export duty revenues; despite losses in some years, it thus acted overall as a taxing mechanism.[51]

The most blatant cases of misuse of the SLPMB's funds occurred under the Albert Margai regime, when, as one of the main sources of liquid cash in the government's control, it was also one of the main loci of corruption. Several cases of misappropriation, discovered by the opposition, were hushed up by the government.[52] Finally in 1966–7, mismanagement reached such a level that it was unable to meet its obligations to producers, and thus provided one of the main grievances against the SLPP government in the 1967 elections.[53] The most obvious case of the use of the Board for political patronage since 1968 has been the appointment to a post in it of Mr Alfred Akibo-Betts, one of the APC's main Freetown organisers. The LPMC, by contrast, appears to have remained free from political pressures.

A comparison of the official buying prices for cocoa, coffee and palm kernels during the late 1960s and early 1970s shows the Liberian Produce Marketing Corporation generally offering rather higher prices than its Sierra Leonean equivalent.[54] In keeping with the differences in their pricing policies, the LPMC cut

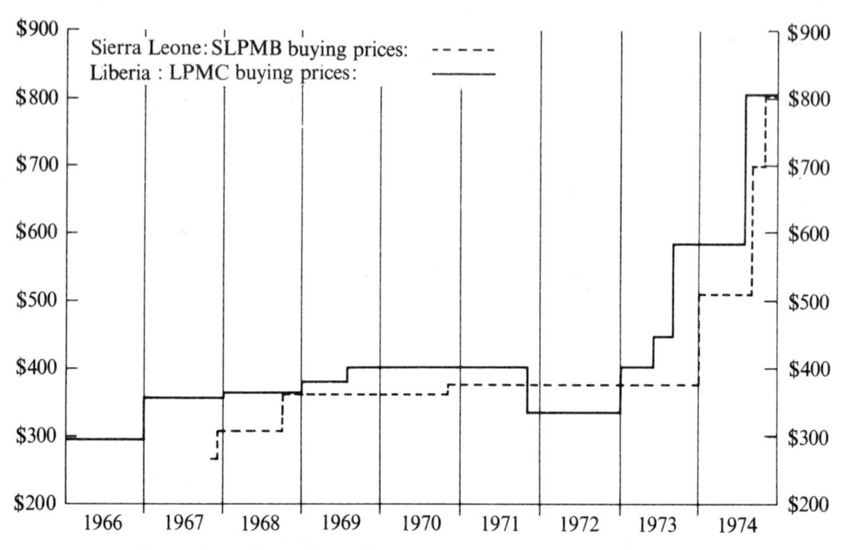

Figure 2. Producer Prices for Cocoa, 1966–74 (in US $ per ton).

Sources for Figures 2–4: Liberia, *Quarterly Statistical Bulletin of Liberia (Summary for 1972)* Table 5.2 (for 1966–72); Liberian Embassy London, and advertised prices in Liberian newspapers (for 1973–4). Sierra Leone, Bank of Sierra Leone, *Annual Report for the Year ended 30th June 1971*, pp. 44–5 (for 1967–71); *Sierra Leone Monthly Trends*, September–October 1971 and January–February 1972 (for 1971–2); Sierra Leone Produce Marketing Board, Freetown and London, personal communications, for 1972–4.

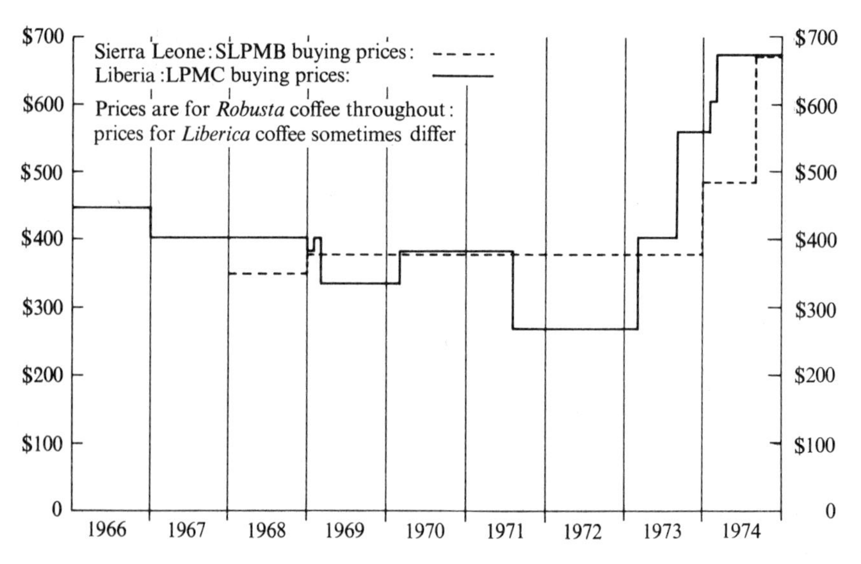

Figure 3. Producer Prices for Coffee, 1966–74 (in US $ per ton).

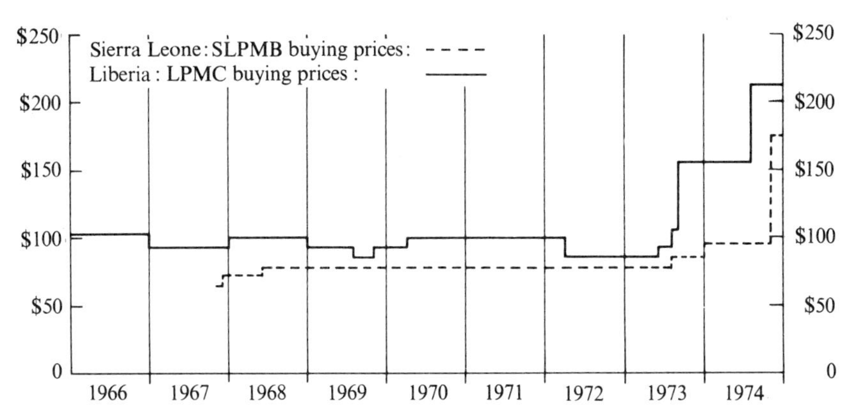

Figure 4. Producer Prices for Palm Kernels, 1966–74 (in US $ per ton).

its producer prices during periods of low world prices for coffee in 1969 and cocoa in 1972, while the SLPMB kept its rates constant; but by the same token, the LPMC was much quicker to offer producers the benefits of the exceptionally high world price levels of 1973. In November 1973, the LPMC was offering $156.75 against the SLPMB's Le71.50 ($85.80) per ton for palm kernels, $582.40 against Le358.40 ($430.08) for cocoa, and $560.00 against Le313.60 ($376.32) for coffee.[55] Not surprisingly, therefore, the produce flowed over the border from Sierra Leone to Liberia, helping to bring about marked increases in the Sierra Leone prices in 1974.[56] The imbalance was even greater with Guinea, where at the same period producers were offered only about a quarter of the Liberian price, and thus had a considerable incentive – despite transport costs and border patrols – to sell their produce in Liberia.[57] Attempts by Guinean producers to escape from low prices and an inconvertible currency have led to smuggling into both Sierra Leone and Liberia, and to consequent problems at the frontiers.[58]

The most striking feature of this comparison is the failure of Sierra Leonean producers to convert their rural voting strength into any ability to gain increased prices for their crops; the sharp price increases of 1974 came at a time when the political bargaining power of the rural areas had been reduced by the APC's electoral monopoly. Unlike cocoa producers in Ghana, they have not formed an economic interest group capable of pressing for political action, despite the opportunities presented by a political structure which gave great scope for factional bargaining. Instead, they have sought to evade SLPMB's pricing policies either by smuggling or by shifting into other areas of the economy: Saylor blames the SLPMB for a decline in the absolute value of Sierra Leonean agricultural produce since 1950, and for a shift within the agricultural sector from cash crops to subsistence farming.[59] Political extraction in Liberia may have the opposite effect: a study in Lofa County refers to the widespread practice of soldiers and other officials demanding subsistence crops such as rice from villagers, and quotes one farmer as switching to export crops since these were less easily looted.[60] The main complaint with export crops was that middlemen, especially Lebanese, paid farmers well below official prices for their produce; the same complaints are heard in Sierra Leone.[61] Overall, though the Guinean comparison shows what difference the political structure can make in producer prices, the differences between Liberia and Sierra Leone in this respect are not nearly so great as the differences in their political systems might lead one to expect.

CONCLUSION

The political economies of Liberia and Sierra Leone for the most part reinforce the patterns of similarity and difference evident in the political system as a whole. Certain basic similarities are obvious, particularly in the overall patterns of production, import and export, and the analogous relationships which these create between two small primary producers and the outside world. In features such as the common dependence on external currencies or dealings with multinational corporations, there is not much to choose between them, though Sierra Leone in each case has acquired a greater symbolic independence through the use of its own national currency and the takeover of a 51% stake in the leading foreign corporation.

Similarities carry over into the domestic political structure, especially through the central role of government, and the opportunities which this provides for those who control political office to increase their access to economic prizes. This has long been a feature of Liberian government, and since independence Sierra Leone has come in some respects to resemble it. The clearest case of this is the exploitation of the Lebanese; in some other respects, such as the establishment by politicians of personal businesses which rely heavily on government for contracts or protected trading, the Sierra Leonean position is still far from the Liberian one, though some individual cases have been noted.

The differences between the two countries, like those in the political system as a whole, derive chiefly from the greater coherence and stability of the Liberian elite. The failure of Sierra Leonean politicians to develop the same business opportunities as their Liberian counterparts can directly be ascribed to various factors, all of which eventually come down to this. One is the persistence – to a muted degree – of norms which prohibit the open use of political office for private gain; even if not fully shared by the would-be gainers, these provide ammunition for their opponents. Another is the uncertainty of political office, the changeover of personnel, and the consequent inability of Sierra Leonean politicians to build up the businesses which have resulted from the long uninterrupted exercise of political power in Liberia. Thirdly, Sierra Leonean politicians with different bases and resources have had an interest in defending these against colleagues and rivals, and hence in preventing them from using some of the opportunities which would have been open to them in Liberia. This is most obviously the case with land-holding in the hinterland.

Against this comparatively greater use of government office for personal advantage in Liberia must be set some countervailing factors. To some extent the differences may be more apparent than real, in that Liberian politicians are well-enough established to make open use of opportunities for self-enrichment which in Sierra Leone may have to be exercised covertly – through bribes, for example, rather than through a private business. Also, Liberia's more impressive record of economic growth may itself partly be due to its political system: to its greater opportunities for central initiative, expressed in Tubman's Open Door Policy; to its greater willingness to collaborate with external investors, expressed by the use of the US dollar as currency, without the need to make the gestures of rhetorical radicalism which have been pressed on Sierra Leonean governments by the need to conciliate their supporters; and to the external confidence resulting from stability itself.

The most difficult problem is in reckoning the extent to which the Sierra Leone system's greater openness to non-elite groups has enabled these to gain economic benefits unavailable in Liberia. The only unequivocal indications are the reservation of hinterland land-holding to the local level in Sierra Leone as against its openness to central penetration in Liberia, and the greater opportunities in Liberia for exploiting involuntary labour. Trades unions are also in a somewhat stronger position in Sierra Leone, and hypothetically it might be argued that illicit diamond miners would have been more strictly controlled had the deposits occurred in Liberia, where they would have had little if any representation. As against that, in the two fields where measurements of comparable returns, however inadequate, are available – iron-ore mining wages and agricultural-produce prices – there are no appreciable differences to the advantage of Sierra Leone, and some to the advantage of Liberia.

The most basic features of the two economies are similar, and insofar as these depend on government decisions, those decisions have been much the same: a convertible currency, a fairly open market system, and a limited role for government. Despite some variations in access to economic prizes among indigenous groups, the common constraints resulting from these features have generally outweighed any differences arising from domestic political structures.

CHAPTER 8

CONCLUDING REVIEW

SIMILARITY AND DIFFERENCE

For all the contrasts between Sierra Leone and Liberia which this essay has been concerned to point out, any comparison of the two countries must start by emphasising their similarities. It is the similarities which make the two countries readily comparable in the first place, placing them in a common context in which differences stand out in such a way that their origins can be located.

These similarities chiefly belong to the first level of political comparison distinguished in the introduction, that of resources. In particular they derive from the resources, common in some degree to all developing countries, which have resulted from western penetration. Firstly, the states themselves were established through external imposition, and thus acquired the administrative apparatus through which this imposition could be managed. Secondly, their economies were drastically reshaped by involvement in the external market, resulting both in the penetration of the internal economy by actors from outside, and in the use of the state apparatus as an intermediary – through its powers of taxation, regulation and produce-marketing – between internal and external producers and markets. Thirdly, the skills and occupations which these political and economic structures called for were such that only a very small proportion of the population could acquire them, and thus attain positions of political influence. The skills were for the most part introduced ones – as lawyers, administrators, army officers – which thus required western education, which was necessarily limited to a few. The institutions and job opportunities which the economy and political structure could support were likewise restricted.

These common features of underdeveloped political systems have been reinforced in Liberia and Sierra Leone. In both countries, local elite groups had special interests in maintaining external connections, rather than mobilising indigenous non-elites; this was true of the Creoles and the Americo-Liberians, and to some extent also of the Sierra Leone Paramount Chiefs. Neither country, too, provided much of a base in educational or economic developments for any radical mass movement in the hinterland, with the single exception of Kono District in Sierra Leone. Hence not only was there no nationalist movement of the kind found in Ghana or Guinea; there was no base even for the ethnic mass parties found in Eastern and Western Nigeria.

These effects of western penetration are quite independent of formal colonial rule. Indeed, they are often more marked in Liberia than in Sierra Leone, where the British through indirect rule and the electoral system bequeathed some counterweights to economic and administrative centralisation. In Liberia, too, the hinterland has been more thoroughly penetrated by big companies in mining or plantation agriculture, and the trading and agricultural enterprises of coastal politicians. But the basic similarities remain. What politics is about in both countries is the competition between those actors who are qualified to be members of an elite, to gain access to the benefits to which, in their view, these qualifications entitle them. Only very secondarily is it about the opportunities for other Sierra Leoneans and Liberians to gain a share in political allocations, and hence about the linkages with elite politicians through which any such opportunities must necessarily be mediated. The period of fairly open electoral competition in Sierra Leone was important more as a means by which a particular section of the elite could project itself into office, than as an occasion for non-elite participation in politics.

Once this point is conceded, the critical question becomes the relationship between potential elite politicians, and the terms on which each of them is admitted to a share in the available prizes. This relationship is itself appreciably affected by resources, and especially by the ethnic cleavages which help to create alliances between politicians in some circumstances, and factional conflict between them in others. This is, however, the area in which rules – the second level of comparison suggested in the Introduction – may have some independent effect.

The experience of Sierra Leone and Liberia suggests that this effect may be marked, in that the countries have sharply contrasting leadership patterns which are only explicable in terms of the differences between the rules left by the colonial government in the one case, and developed by the coastal community in the other. One aspect of this is the difference, already sufficiently emphasised, between the resource holders admitted to high office in the two systems. The highest positions in the Liberian one have consistently been monopolised by members of leading Americo-Liberian families, just as (though only in party political office and then to a rather lesser extent) they have been monopolised in Sierra Leone by those who combined a hinterland electoral base with the educational or professional qualifications needed to hold office in Freetown. Certainly many Creoles have reached ministerial office in Sierra Leone, just as tribal men have in Liberia, but in each case they have done so by associating themselves with the individuals and institutions of the dominant group; with the Margais or Stevens and an electoral coalition in the one case, or with Tubman or Tolbert and the Masons or TWP in the other. The main difference between the two countries in this respect is that whereas the Sierra Leonean system has incorporated social groups into politics, through electoral coalitions or other institutions, in Liberia incorporation has been confined to individuals. Liberian hinterlanders have been recruited in large numbers, especially when account is taken of local recruitment in the County administrations, but this has been on condition that they mobilise no hinterland or ethnic identity.

A second and related contrast is between the coherence or fragmentation of the governing groups which result. The relationship between this and the rules of the two systems has equally been emphasised at many points in earlier chapters. Especially worth noting is the way in which the Liberian rules push would-be political participants either towards acceptance of the rules and the maximisation of personal opportunities within them or else towards the much riskier strategy of waiting (or working) for a substantial change, whereas the Sierra Leonean ones allow much more scope for manoeuvring on the edges of a rule structure which is vastly more uncertain. The difference between the continuity and stability of political institutions in Liberia, and the Sierra Leonean dogfights between party, military, bureaucratic and other factions is one side of the contrast; the other is the possibility of political change in Liberia of a more radical kind than Sierra Leone seems likely to experience.

The opportunities for non-elite groups to participate in politics are related to these contrasts in elite relationships. Of them all, only the illicit diamond miners of Kono are in a strong enough position to ensure that the government takes account of their interests, since they directly control an economic resource which is important both to the national economy and to individual politicians' prospects of enrichment. Other non-elite economic interests are not dealt with very differently in the two countries, since in neither case are they of vital interest to government. Iron ore mineworkers and cash crop producers appear to be treated much the same in Liberia and Sierra Leone though with some indications in each case that the Liberians may be better off. As against that, Liberians are more likely to be forcibly recruited for work in plantation agriculture, and Liberian trade unions are brought more closely under government control. Both governments have responded very similarly to demands for indigenisation, though the Sierra Leonean one – in its sporadic expulsions of Foulahs, for instance – has felt it necessary to take more account of the petty trading sector.

The main differences in handling non-elite demands arise in local government, where they are related on the one hand to Sierra Leonean electoral factions, and on the other to the Liberian County system and fear of hinterland political mobilisation. Hence factions formed over chieftaincy disputes and other local issues tend in Sierra Leone to attach themselves to rival political brokers; these brokers may belong to different national political parties, or to the same one (as with Mende factions in the SLPP before 1967), or one may support the government while the other lies low in the hope of a change of regime (as has tended to happen since 1970). In Liberia, where their opportunities for making themselves heard are in any case much less, such local disputes tend to be mediated by the County Superintendent, or through patrons such as local landowners, Representatives or the President himself.

Since the Sierra Leonean rules were decisively affected by the colonial power, one might expect independence to lead eventually to a reorientation of rules so that they more accurately reflected indigenous resources, and thus converged with the Liberian ones. To some extent this has happened. The most marked change in Sierra Leone politics since independence has been the increase in the capacity of governing groups to use those resources implicit in western penetration which had previously been monopolised by the colonial power – notably control of coercion and economic transactions – in order to restrict the resources derived from local level support. This has been as true of civilian as of military regimes. The suppression of opposition groups and the use of state power to provide wealth for politicians both provide evidence for this convergence. In neither respect has Sierra Leone yet gone as far as Liberia, but this may merely be because elite fragmentation has created constraints which have not yet been fully overcome, and which Liberian politicians do not have to reckon with.

In other respects, the effects of colonial rule are longer lived. The colonial power was not only a resource in itself; it also helped to mobilise indigenous resources which have not been brought into politics – at any rate in the same way – in Liberia. This is especially true of ethnicity. Further, though the rules bequeathed at independence held the seeds of their own decay, no comprehensive and generally accepted alternative has been developed to replace them; this has left room for other resources, such as the Sierra Leone army and paramilitary forces trained by foreign instructors, to be brought into play. Here, by contrast, it is Sierra Leone which has, as it were, taken the lead; these resources are equally implicit in the social and institutional structure of Liberia, where eventually the rules will presumably need to be changed or adapted to accommodate them. So in some respects, Liberia is tomorrow's Sierra Leone: in others, Sierra Leone is tomorrow's Liberia.

To put it another way, neither Sierra Leone nor Liberia has yet experienced the 'green uprising' which for Huntington leads to the integration of rural participation and central leadership through a set of effective institutions.[1] But the critical relationship between participation and institutionalisation is very different in the two countries. For Sierra Leone, the 'praetorian' polity in Huntington's terms, the prospects for stable and effective government depend on devising acceptable institutional arrangements through which to incorporate already mobilised resources into political life. For Liberia, the 'contained' one, they depend on the capacity of existing institutions gradually to adapt themselves and extend their scope so as to incorporate new resources.

In neither case are the prospects very promising. In Sierra Leone, there is no formula in sight to replace that provided – however temporarily and inadequately – by the colonial power. The various political party regimes, including the present one, have been little more than clusters of cliques awaiting their chance of a share in the spoils; none of them have possessed the dynamic – the ideology, if you will – needed to provide coherence and a sense of purpose to the government, and a formula for reconciliation to its opponents. The military, too, has been tried and has failed. The present APC regime, or some alternative, may manage to remain in power, with a greater or lesser stiffening of external paramilitary support, but there is little sense even of nationalism on which to build a new concept of legitimacy.

Liberia appears to present a much less depressing picture. The political system appears to be not only stable and institutionalised, as evidenced by the crises of succession which Liberia has surmounted, whereas Sierra Leone has failed to do so; it also has some capacity to extend its scope to incorporate an increasing range of people from outside the original coastal core. Admittedly, the methods by which it maintains itself are not always those which liberal academics approve; but political systems need to be maintained, after all, and there is no reason to suppose that the most effective means for doing it will necessarily coincide with liberal concepts of justice or indeed with elementary honesty.

The basic problems are two. Firstly, there is the problem of organisation: whether it is possible to extend indefinitely the essentially personal networks of family and patronage through which individuals (rather than social groups or interests) are currently assimilated to the core. It may be taken as given that continued extension will be necessary, simply in order to meet the expectations of those whom education and economic change are bringing into a position to participate in politics. The capacities of personal networks to do this are limited, not so much by the numbers which they can incorporate (which may be manageable in a country as small as Liberia) but by the range of social groups and political demands. Once a sizeable number of people become discontented with the politics of jobbery in which the present system largely consists, some structural transformation will become necessary. There is nothing to show whether the Liberian leadership – which has so far proved extremely astute in accommodating itself to change – will be able to manage this further metamorphosis.

Secondly, there is the problem of identity. The Huntingtonian ideal which sees participation gradually extending through an established core of institutions, requires that this process should not come up against any unbridgeable fault-lines in the population.[2] This, indeed, is part of what is meant by institutional 'autonomy'. In Liberia, the obvious fault-line between the Americo-Liberian and tribal elements has already been partly bridged by intermarriage and assimilation, by political patronage, and to some extent by a sense of Liberian identity – much more noticeable than any sense of Sierra Leonean identity – which is not simply coterminous with the core. Nonetheless, as participation expands, it will become increasingly tempting for hinterland politicians to seek to promote their interests by mobilising latent hinterland or tribal identities against the core. This might be managed either through hinterland political parties or through a section of the military, and it might come as a response to organisational inadequacies revealed by the failure of personal patronage networks.

In both countries, though in different ways, the integration of resources and rules, of the social forces which give rise to mobilisation and the political arrangements which are necessary to contain it, gives rise to strains which are unlikely to be easily overcome. With this in mind, it is time to go back to some of the general problems of political comparison with which this essay started.

COMPARISON REVISITED

No complete or definitive approach to political comparison is possible. For all the enthusiasm with which the devotees of a science of comparative politics have urged on their supporters, the essential theoretical obstacles to the enterprise remain unshaken. First, there is the problem of information, since the collection of the information needed to sustain a comparative political science raises theoretical and not merely practical problems relating to the nature of meaningful behaviour and the language in which it is to be described. Second, there is the problem of comparability, which places insuperable difficulties in the way of transferring descriptive concepts – voting behaviour, political parties, military coups – from one setting to another. Third, there is the problem of priority, since any approach to comparison carries with it implicit assumptions of importance which can ultimately be justified only in normative terms. Each of these basic problems, as I see them, contains a cluster of further difficulties: of causation, measurement, conceptual language, and so forth. Since there is no place here to go into the argument in the detail it requires, I shall have to content myself with what is, essentially, a statement of personal conviction: there is no science of comparative politics waiting to be discovered.

But abandoning the more pretentious claims for political comparison is no grounds for abandoning the activity altogether. An appreciation of its limitations is necessary to understand its value. This lies in uncovering and systematising the common features which underlie political activity. That such common features exist is undeniable. It is these that make the work of Aristotle and Machiavelli still relevant and illuminating to modern politics, and provide the basis for the varied 'approaches' devised by modern political scientists. Hence the pursuit of common elements in politics, and of the differences which the use of a common framework for analysis is necessary to uncover, is essential for a full (or even adequate) understanding of individual political arrangements. Comparative politics is not the potential science which MacIntyre derides, but neither is it the activity analogous to the study of hole-digging which he unkindly suggests.[3]

If this activity is to get beyond the rule of thumb stage, it is necessary to construct models of political interaction, which enable one to bring together as much as possible of the relevant and available data, and show the connections between elements in it. Such models are not true or false; they are simply more or less useful. Insofar as the connections which they indicate carry conviction, they may be regarded as explanations, remembering always that several different explanations, drawn up in relation to different models, may be available for the same range of information. Any application of the same model to two or more sets of information, similarly, generates a comparison.

A great deal therefore depends on the choice of model. In my view, some kinds of model are very much more useful than others. First, it is essential to use a model which will correlate information at a *systemic* level – at the level, that is to say, of the whole social order which one is seeking to explain, rather than that of the actors or groups within it. This level may be that of the whole globe, or that of the village; in most comparative studies, like this one, it will be the state, though with adequate means for taking account of international influences. Any subsystemic approach runs into intense comparability problems, since the behaviour of subsystemic actors is conditioned to an important extent by the system within which they act. Voting, for example, does not mean the same thing in Liberia and Sierra Leone, any more than it means the same thing in England and Northern Ireland. Hence any comparison of subsystemic activities should be undertaken by relating each action to its role within the system in which it is performed.

Second, it is, I think, useful to abandon the attempt to demarcate boundaries between a construct known as 'the political system' and other elements in society. If one is attempting to devise a *science* of comparative politics in systemic terms, then it is necessary to build a 'real' or 'homeostatic' system whose boundaries and structures are precisely defined, so that it is possible to measure the flow of transactions through it, and monitor their effects. This enterprise creates great difficulties, which have not been overcome.[4] If, as I have argued, a science of comparative politics is impossible anyhow, then one is better off with a more flexible, non-homeostatic concept of system which does not require any demarcation between political and non-political elements, and which enables one to call on any information which seems relevant to the range of events which one is seeking to explain.

Thirdly, it is necessary to devise some means for relating explanations at a systemic level to the behaviour of subsystemic actors and groups, and to the concepts which are used to explain this. The two most commonly used models for systemic explanation, Eastonian systems analysis and structural-functionalism, are especially weak in this respect. Both of them are geared to the adaptive and dispute-solving activities of government. They have no concepts for explaining how and why the demands arise which government must deal with, except to a very limited extent through the idea of 'feedback'. This again is partly the result of an artificial distinction between the 'political system' and the 'society' in which the society is treated largely as a given. Marxism does very much better, by relating individual economic behaviour to political groupings and consequent systemic outcomes. For my purpose in this essay, however, it insists on analytic categories – such as class – and on systemic relationships – such as economic determinism – which largely beg the questions which I am interested in asking.

The model used in this essay has been devised, in a fairly rough-and-ready form, to meet these problems of comparison. It sees the political system as an arena for conflict, and the configuration of conflict within it as the most important characteristic which structures the behaviour of individual actors. This configuration is derived from the combination of resources with rules, both of which are exploited by the actors, who are motivated to seek the prizes which the system offers them, or could possibly be made to offer them. In this way, the systemic and individual levels of explanation are brought closely into harmony. Explanations of individual behaviour are offered by showing how it might be considered rational for an actor in a given environment, seeking particular prizes, to act in the way he did. Explanations of systemic developments are offered by tracing the effects of this behaviour on a set of resources which may be taken as given, and a set of rules which is partly given.

This model does not, of course, overcome the basic problems of political comparison. No model could. Its usefulness, like that of any other model, is to be judged by its success in drawing the varied elements of politics in the cases it examines into a coherent and convincing relationship. This in turn depends on the plausibility of the priorities which it implies, and on the adequacy of its main concepts. This question of priorities, as I suggested earlier, is essentially a normative one; it is a question of what politics is *about*, which can to some extent be derived from (and must in any case be made to fit) the activities of the actors, but which also depends on the judgement of the observer. The model used here tends to emphasise the means by which politicians *gain* power, and the uses of their social environment in helping them to do so, rather than the ways in which they may *use* power, and the effect of purposive government action on the social environment itself. It emphasises competition for essentially personal or sectarian prizes such as wealth and government office, rather than possible attempts to implement general moral or ideological goals. There is some justification for this emphasis. For one thing, some access to – or at least active desire for – political prizes is essential to a politician's existence: without it, he is not a politician. This does not entail that the pursuit of power is a politician's main or only goal: he may acquire it without really fighting for it, by heredity or acclamation. But most politicians are actively concerned in seeking prizes such as office, which are essential for whatever other ends they wish to achieve. For another thing, this emphasis does in fact appear to coincide fairly closely with the practice of politics in both Liberia and Sierra Leone. There is much developmental rhetoric in both countries, but this is the common currency of third world politicians, and is generally treated with scepticism by its hearers. There has never been, in either country, any national movement directed towards developmental goals which has sought to displace the politics of personal advancement by that of communal ideals. Nor has any national leader in the period covered by this study left office by any other means than death or forcible ejection. Certainly some politicians are much more honest than others. But however disheartening it may be, the characterisation of politics as a struggle for benefits seems to me to be adequate.

The model as it stands would clearly need to be adapted in order to be able to compare political processes in situations where this characterisation did not hold good.

A second assumption implicit in the model is rationality: that politicians have consistent sets of goals, and choose a course of action designed to maximise their achievement of these goals at the lowest possible cost in expendable resources. The application of this assumption is difficult. At its weakest, it may merely mean that an actor should be able to produce some kind of reason for his actions; in this sense it can scarcely be used to explain such actions at all. At its strongest, it requires resources, goals and possible alternatives to be codified and quantified in such a way that the most rational course of action can be logically deduced; this is impossible in practical life since goals and alternatives cannot be fully specified, and information is invariably incomplete. In practice, too, politicians will have differing and changing perceptions of the opportunities open to them, and of the courses of action which they should consequently pursue. Both Albert Margai and Siaka Stevens may be regarded as seeking the goal of an executive presidency which would mark their supremacy over other actors in Sierra Leone politics: the different ways in which they went about trying to achieve this goal may be ascribed partly to the circumstances in which each of them operated, but partly also to different skills or perceptions which are scarcely separable from the idea of rationality itself. When it came to the point, Stevens was better at achieving his goals than Albert Margai. Nonetheless, there is a continuum between the two extremes noted above. It is possible to show that actors with their eye on easily discernible prizes such as political office would be more likely to follow one course of action than another under given circumstances; and the more clearly the circumstances can be codified, the more useful will the resulting explanation be. For a Liberian middle-ranking politician, for example, it scarcely seems worthwhile to stay out of politics in tacit opposition to the present regime, in the hope that upheavals in Monrovia will bring one back to power, and the best option therefore appears to be to associate oneself with government on whatever terms one can get; for a Sierra Leonean in a comparable position the prospects of gaining through an upheaval in Freetown seem vastly more promising. Of course, these expectations may prove in the light of hindsight to have been misleading, as much in one case as in the other; but any concept of rationality must be based on the prospects discernible at the moment a decision is made, and the calculation of these prospects provides scope for the skills which themselves prevent rationality from ever being fully codified.

Finally, the model depends on the conceptual usefulness and practical applicability of the twin concepts resources and rules. Their usefulness in tying together the social forces with which politics is concerned and the procedures through which it operates has, I hope, been sufficiently demonstrated by the preceding chapters. Their application to actual situations has equally been demonstrated, though in the process the impossibility of measuring resources, of fully defining rules, and thus of deriving testable causal hypotheses from the relationships between them, has become apparent. Certainly some resources can, in a sense, be measured: economic resources, in cash; military capacity, in firepower popular support, in votes. But these measurements do not indicate the effective *political* worth of the resources concerned, and they are of value only in comparing resources of a similar kind. Any measurements of different resources on a comparable scale requires a set of rules which allot values to each particular kind of resource. Even this is a tricky enterprise, because the prizes open to the holders of some resources may not coincide with those competed for by the holders of others. In the British political system, for example, the political parties compete in electoral terms for seats in the House of Commons and control of the Cabinet; but no equivalent rules exist for competition between the Cabinet, trades union leaders, and senior civil servants. Measurement of their relative resources becomes still more problematical when the rules themselves are liable to change. Rules are procedural practices, which may be maintained by consensus or legitimacy, by enforcement by those who profit from them, or by the prudence of participants. It is clear from the number of rule changes noted in earlier chapters that they have no claim to permanence. They are simply codifications of current practice, and when the practice changes – when Stevens imprisoned UDP leaders without parliamentary authority in 1970, for example – so does the rule. It is tempting to postulate some 'real' distribution of underlying social power between resources, which the rules currently in force may reflect to a greater or lesser extent. Certainly it seems plausible to say that a particular set of rules may break down because it fails to give adequate weight to a potentially powerful resource, which consequently enforces a new set of rules: the 1974 military takeover in Ethiopia, or a Marxist revolution, may both be seen in this way. But a distribution of power independent of rules is, like Locke's concept of real essences, beyond the possibility of observation.

These problems of emphasis and definition are forms of the general problems of information, comparability and priority which limit any approach to political comparison, and which ultimately derive from the nature of political activity itself. They therefore call for no special apology: any other approach would contain the same limitations in one form or another. More is to be gained by conceding them and working within them than by trying to explain them away. What emerges from the model is a set of categories – a method rather than a theory – which can be applied to any political system, whether international, national or subnational, which is characterised by internal competition in pursuit of prizes. The value of comparing systems will then depend on the extent to which they share common features which make them worth comparison. Political comparison in this sense may be a modest enterprise, but it is one which has been little attempted, and which it is well worth trying.

STATISTICAL APPENDIX

1. Area and population

		Liberia				Sierra Leone		
Area (sq.km.)			111,369	(1)			71,740	(1)
Total population								
At last census			(1962) 1,016,443	(1)			(1963) 2,180,355	(1)
1970 estimate			1,171,000	(1)			2,550,000	(1)
Density of population								
1970 estimate (per sq.km.)			10.5				35.5	
Population of capital								
At last census	Monrovia		(1962) 80,992	(1)	Freetown		(1963) 127,917	(1)
1970 estimate	Monrovia		96,226	(1)	Freetown		178,600	(1)
Other towns over 10,000								
At last census	Harbel, Mont.		31,730	(2)	Bo Town, Bo		26,613	(3)
	Buchanan, Gd. Bassa		11,909	(2)	Kenema Town, Ken.		13,246	(3)
					Kissi, W.A.		13,143	(3)
					Makeni, Bombali		12,304	(3)
					Lunsar, P. Loko		12,132	(3)
					Koidu, Kono		11,706	(3)
Urbanisation								
% in towns over 10,000			12.3				10.0	
Principal ethnic groups								
at last census (total and percentage)	Kpelle	211,081	20.8	(2)	Mende	672,831	30.9	(3)
	Bassa	165,856	16.3		Temne	648,931	29.8	
	Gio	83,208	8.2		Limba	183,496	8.4	
	Kru	80,813	7.6		Kono	104,573	4.8	
	Grebo	77,007	7.6		Koranko	80,732	3.7	
	Mano	72,122	7.1		Bullom	74,674	3.4	
	Loma	53,891	5.3		Susu	67,288	3.1	
	Krahn	52,552	5.2		Foulah	66,824	3.1	
	Gola	47,295	4.7		Loko	64,459	3.0	
	Kissi	34,914	3.4		Mandingo	51,024	2.3	
	Mandingo	29,750	2.9		Kissi	48,954	2.2	
	Vai	28,898	2.8		Yalunka	15,005	0.7	
	Gbandi	28,599	2.8					
	Americo	6,452	0.6*		Creole	41,783	1.9	

Sources

(1) *United Nations Demographic Yearbook 1970.*
(2) Liberia, *1962 Census of Population.*
(3) Sierra Leone, *1963 Census of Population.*

* The figure for Americo-Liberians has been reached by subtracting the total for non-tribal aliens in the 1962 census from the total non-tribal population; this equals the figure gained by subtracting the total for tribal Liberians (984,120) from the total for Liberian citizens (990,572); several authors have followed Liebenow, *op. cit.* p. 222 in counting the non-tribal total of 23,478 as referring only to Liberian citizens (i.e. Americo-Liberians). This is a point of some political importance.

Both Sierra Leone and Liberia conducted censuses in 1974, full results of which were not available at the time of going to press. Provisional totals for Liberia were 1,496,000, and for Sierra Leone just over 3,000,000; Monrovia's population was 180,000, and Freetown's 274,000.

2. *Economic indices*

NB. Sierra Leone figures are given in most publications in Leones; in this appendix, they have throughout been converted to US dollars, at an exchange rate of Le1.00 = $1.40 up to and including 1967, and Le1.00 = $1.20 thereafter.

Gross domestic product at purchasers' values		*Liberia*		*Sierra Leone*	
		Total	*Per cap.*	*Total*	*Per cap.*
	1960	$220m	$223		
	1963	$274m	$266	$303m	$132
	1967	330m	297	391m	160
	1968	352m	311	389m	157
	1969	397m	345	443m	176
	1970	417m	357	451m	177
	1971	438m	368		

Source: *United Nations Statistical Yearbook*, 1971, p. 600; 1972, p. 627; 1973, p. 596. Figures for GDP must be treated with great caution, since several different measurements are available, and figures from different sources vary widely even for what is ostensibly the same measurement; the figures above are those which have the greatest chance of comparing like with like.

National income (net national product)		*Total*	*Per cap.*	*Total*	*Per cap.*
	1963			$295.1m	$128.1
	1966	$191.9m	$176.1	$361.2m	$150.5
	1967	199.8m	179.8	353.9m	144.8
	1968	210.2m	185.7	348.6m	140.7
	1969	238.6m	207.3	397.4m	157.9
	1970	253.1m	216.7	401.9m	157.7
	1971	259.1m	217.7		

Sources: for Sierra Leone (national income at market prices), *United Nations Yearbook of National Accounts Statistics*, 1972, Vol. II, p. 240; for Liberia (national income at factor cost), *Quarterly Statistical Bulletin of Liberia Summary for 1972*, Table 1.2; per capita figures obtained in each case by dividing totals by United Nations population estimates.

Consumer prices. (Index to base year 1965)			
	1963		85.8
	1964	98.3	95.7
	1965	100.0	100.0
	1966	103.2	104.4
	1967	108.9	109.5
	1968	111.6	111.0
	1969	123.1	114.7
	1970	124.0	123.4
	1971	124.3	120.5
	1972	129.2	125.2
	1973		130.7

Source: *United Nations Yearbook of Labour Statistics* 1973, pp. 700–1; Sierra Leone figures recalculated to base year 1965.

		Liberia	*Sierra Leone*
Index of GDP per capita at constant prices			
	1964		92.2
	1965		96.8
	1966	100.0	100.0
	1967	99.1	96.7
	1968	100.6	96.0
	1969	100.3	102.3
	1970	102.1	105.7
	1971	104.6	

Sources: for Sierra Leone, *Sierra Leone Annual Statistical Digest 1971*, Table 82, recalculated to base year 1966; for Liberia, GDP at market prices from *Quarterly Statistical Bulletin, op. cit.*, Table 1.1, divided by United Nations population estimates and consumer price index, indexed to base year 1966.

GDP by sector						
As % of total GDP	*1965*	*1967*	*1969*	*1965*	*1967*	*1969*
Agriculture, etc.	28.6	25.7	21.0	32.7	41.1	36.4
Mining	32.8	31.1	30.8	20.1	15.5	19.5
Manufacturing	3.9	4.7	4.1	6.6	6.3	6.2
Construction	4.0	6.6	4.8	3.8	4.1	4.7
Trade	9.0	10.4	16.5	15.8	13.7	13.4
Transport	6.0	5.8	6.7	8.1	8.3	8.6
Insurance etc.	0.9	0.9	1.0	1.0	0.9	1.3
Social services	4.8	5.5	1.8	3.6	3.6	3.4
Government services	9.4	9.3	13.4	5.4	5.5	5.6

Source: *United Nations Yearbook of National Accounts Statistics*, 1971, Vol. II, pp. 3, 294; 1972, Vol. II, p. 3, converted to percentages.

Employment by sector at latest census, as % of active population	(1962)	(1963)
Agriculture	80.9	74.8
Mining	3.5	5.1
Commerce	2.8	5.7
Manufacturing	2.1	4.4
Services	6.0	3.1

Source: *United Nations Yearbook of Labour Statistics*, 1973, pp. 47, 53.

Total exports by value (In US $)			
	1965		88,513,000
	1966	144,039,100	82,685,000
	1967	140,630,000	70,755,000
	1968	158,298,000	95,654,000
	1969	188,934,500	108,098,000
	1970	203,725,500	101,460,000
	1971	213,452,900	100,060,000
	1972	232,708,400	

Sources: *Sierra Leone Annual Statistical Digest 1971*, Table 65; *Quarterly Statistical Bulletin, op. cit.*, Table 4.1. Liberian totals are for the sum of 'major exports'.

	Liberia			*Sierra Leone*		
Composition of exports						
By value, as % of total	*1967*	*1969*	*1971*	*1967*	*1969*	*1971*
Coffee	1.8	1.3	1.9	0.7	3.5	4.2
Cocoa	0.4	0.8	0.6	3.2	3.3	3.3
Palm kernels	1.3	0.8	1.0	2.4	6.2	7.2
Rubber	10.8	16.1	15.2			
Logs		3.7	3.4			
Diamonds	3.8	4.7	2.6	62.3	71.0	60.9
Iron ore	81.9	72.5	75.2	19.8	11.2	13.9

Sources: *ibid*., Tables 65 and 70 and Table 4.1.

Destination of exports				
By value, as % of total	*1976*	*1969*	*1971*	*1971*
Africa				0.6
America	31.0	28.8	23.1	6.7
(USA)	(29.9)	(27.7)	(22.2)	(6.5)
Asia	1.2	6.6	11.4	7.3
(Japan)	(1.1)	(6.3)	(11.0)	(6.8)
Europe	66.2	63.7	64.3	82.6
(UK)	(18.9)	(5.7)	(3.5)	(62.8)
(W. Germany)	(28.0)	(23.2)	(18.5)	(5.5)
(Netherlands)	(5.0)	(9.0)	(15.0)	(9.4)
(Italy)	(11.1)	(8.6)	(12.8)	

Sources: *ibid*., Table 67 and Table 4.6.

Government domestic revenue
(In US $m)

1966	46.7m	
1967	48.1m	53.2m
1968	51.8m	46.7m
1969	61.8m	61.3m
1970	66.5m	67.9m
1971	69.9m	64.2m
1972	78.1m	

Sources: *ibid*., Table 88 and Table 2.3.

Composition of domestic revenue,
as % of total

	1967	*1969*	*1971*	*1967*	*1969*	*1971*
Direct taxes	40.5	42.7	41.5	21.1	24.6	28.6
(Rubber concessions)	(15.6)	(13.8)	(10.6)			
(Iron ore profits)	(20.8)	(19.4)	(17.5)			
Indirect taxes	49.0	43.5	44.2	64.2	66.6	60.6
(Import duties)	(33.5)	(27.7)	(28.2)	(50.9)	(49.6)	(36.0)
(Export duties)	(1.7)	(2.3)	(1.1)	(7.4)	(8.3)	(7.7)
Other revenues	10.5	13.8	14.3	14.7	8.8	10.8

Sources: *ibid*.

Composition of government expenditure, as % of total	*Liberia* 1967	*Liberia* 1969	*Sierra Leone* 1967	*Sierra Leone* 1969
General services	31.7	33.1	24.2	24.0
(General administration)	(20.1)	(22.7)	(12.1)	(10.2)
(Justice and police)	(3.9)	(3.8)	(5.6)	(6.4)
(Defence)	(4.3)	(5.0)	(4.2)	(5.4)
Social services	35.1	35.3	28.2	26.9
(Education)	(17.7)	(16.2)	(18.1)	(17.6)
(Health)	(9.2)	(10.9)	(7.1)	(6.5)
Economic services	24.3	21.6	25.4	22.6
(Agriculture)	(2.0)	(1.7)	(5.6)	(3.1)
(Communications)	(13.9)	(9.4)	(7.2)	(8.8)
Pensions			4.3	3.9
Debt service charges	8.4	10.4	17.8	22.5
Total current expenditure	$76.1m	66.5m	$51.0m	50.7m

Sources: *ibid*., Table 89 and Table 2.4.

BIBLIOGRAPHICAL NOTE

Neither Sierra Leone nor Liberia has been very well covered by academic research, and for Liberia the material is especially thin. This brief note is intended only to draw attention to some of the principal sources, and to indicate some of the more obvious gaps in the material.

The standard texts for the politics of Sierra Leone are Martin Kilson's *Political Change in a West African State* and John Cartwright's *Politics in Sierra Leone 1947–1967*. Kilson's is a study of relationships between colonial rulers and indigenous people since 1896, and does not go far beyond independence. Its underlying theme, that indigenous elites acquire interests in common with the colonial power and opposed to those of the masses, has an importance well beyond its applicability to Sierra Leone; it also pays more attention than Cartwright to local politics in the hinterland, and especially to the relationship between chiefs and people. In other respects, especially on central politics, Cartwright's book is far more detailed and thorough, and takes the story up to the fall of Sir Albert Margai in 1967; while Kilson's theme is elite exploitation, Cartwright's is the survival of a fairly open, bargaining democratic style of politics. The NRC regime is discussed in Bebler's *Military Rule in Africa*, and in Fisher's article, 'Elections and Coups in Sierra Leone'. There is as yet no adequate study of the APC government, but Victor King's doctoral thesis, currently nearing completion at the University of Manchester, should help to fill this gap.

For Liberia, virtually the only book in the field is J. Gus Liebenow's *Liberia, The Evolution of Privilege*, which expands and updates his earlier surveys in Gwendolen Carter's *African One-Party States*, and James Coleman & Carl Rosberg, *Political Parties and National Integration in Tropical Africa*. This surveys the whole field from history, social change and economic development to central politics, hinterland relations, and foreign affairs, and is inevitably far less detailed than equivalent work on Sierra Leone; it tends also to adopt the carping tone characteristic of much work on Liberia, which derives from an implicit comparison of Liberian reality with either the dynamic rhetoric of newly independent states or with the western liberal pretensions of the Liberian regime itself. That apart, it is a model of its kind. Martin Lowenkopf's thesis, *Political Modernization and Integration in Liberia*, also covers a very broad field and therefore duplicates much of Liebenow's work, but contains useful information especially on central politics.

On local politics, two excellent theses exist for Sierra Leone in Walter Barrows' *Local-level Politics in Sierra Leone*, and Victor Minikin's *Local Politics in Kono District*; Roger Tangri's book on *Local Government and Politics in Sierra Leone*, currently in preparation, promises to extend their scope with a more general survey including data from the Northern Province. Local politics in Liberia, by contrast, is still an open field.

Social and economic change is one area in which the Liberian data matches or surpasses the Sierra Leonean. The study of the Liberian economy by the team from Northwestern University, published as *Growth without Development*, is in parts unjustifiably hostile but provides a wealth of information. R. G. Saylor's *The Economic System of Sierra Leone* is a much shorter but still useful work. On social change Merran Fraenkel's *Tribe and Class in Monrovia* is especially worth mentioning. Finally, J. I. Clarke's *Sierra Leone in Maps* and S. von Gnielinski's *Liberia in Maps* are both very useful compilations, though the Sierra Leonean volume has a much more detailed coverage.

NOTES

Chapter 1. Political Comparison

1. To take a West African example, Philip Foster and A. R. Zolberg's recent collection, *Ghana and the Ivory Coast* (Chicago 1971) contains two excellent chapters closely comparing economic processes in the two countries, yet its political coverage is divided into two chapters on Ghana and another two on the Ivory Coast: comparison disappears.
2. These are two of the extremes compared in G. A. Almond & G. B. Powell, *Comparative Politics: A Developmental Approach* (Little Brown 1966) p. 217.
3. This conception of politics is as old as Aristotle, and underlies such modern texts as J. D. B. Miller, *The Nature of Politics* (Penguin 1962) and S. E. Finer, *Comparative Government* (Penguin 1970). However, I owe a particular debt, for inspiring the concepts used in this book, to F. G. Bailey, *Stratagems and Spoils* (Blackwell 1969), and to M. Staniland, 'Single-party Regimes and Political Change', in C. Leys, ed., *Politics and Change in Developing Countries* (Cambridge 1969).
4. Thomas Hobbes, *De Cive*.
5. At the level of grand development theory, this difference is reflected in the divergence of approach between Barrington Moore, *Social Origins of Dictatorship and Democracy: Lord and Peasant in the Making of the Modern World* (Beacon 1966), who emphasises the role of economic relationships in creating different types of regime, and Samuel Huntington, *Political Order in Changing Societies* (Yale 1968) who emphasises the role of political leadership patterns and institutions.
6. This is no place to go fully into the arguments on this subject; for a persuasive statement of the case against a 'science' of comparative politics, see Alasdair MacIntyre, 'Is a Science of Comparative Politics Possible?', in *Against the Self-Images of the Age* (Duckworth 1971).

Chapter 2. Historical Summary

1. For detailed figures, see the Statistical Appendix.
2. The histories of Liberia and Sierra Leone can be viewed from either of two perspectives: that of the indigenous societies, on which there first impinged alien coastal settlements, and was later imposed an alien rule; or that of the coastal settlements themselves, and their extension of control over the hinterland. The justification for taking the latter viewpoint is that this is closest to the process by which the central political structures of the two countries developed.
3. There are several works on the history of the Creole community in Sierra Leone, notably C. Fyfe, *A History of Sierra Leone* (Oxford 1962), J.

Peterson, *Province of Freedom: A History of Sierra Leone 1787–1870* (Northwestern 1969) and A. T. Porter, *Creoledom: A Study of the Development of Freetown Society* (Oxford 1963); for Liberia, there still appears to be no successor to H. Johnston, *Liberia* (Hutchinson 1906).

4. This is a familiar feature of supposedly traditional classifications; see S. Huntington, *op. cit.*, p. 38, and for Liberia, W. L. d'Azevedo, 'Some Historical Problems in the Delineation of a Central West Atlantic Region', *Annals of the New York Academy of Sciences*, vol. 96, pp. 512–38, 1962.
5. Information on the distribution of the various ethnic groups is most readily available in J. I. Clarke, *Sierra Leone in Maps* (University of London 1966) and S. von Gnielinski, *Liberia in Maps* (University of London 1972); see also Map C and the Statistical Appendix.
6. For central Liberia, see R. Fulton, *The Kpelle: A Study of Political Change in the Interior of Liberia* (Ph.D. Dissertation, University of Connecticut 1969), ch. 5.
7. In Liberia, only about 0.6%; see the Statistical Appendix.
8. For past and present administrative divisions, see Clarke, *op. cit.*, pp. 28–33.
9. Gnielinski, *op. cit.*, pp. 32–7.
10. *Quarterly Statistical Bulletin of Liberia, Summary for 1972* (Monrovia, Ministry of Planning 1973) Table 4.
11. Sierra Leone, *Annual Statistical Digest 1971* (Freetown, Central Statistics Office 1972) Tables 65, 71, 72.
12. R. W. Clower *& al.*, *Growth without Development, An Economic Survey of Liberia* (Northwestern 1966) p. 23.
13. The figures compared are for Gross Domestic Product at Purchasers' Values, in *United Nations Statistical Yearbook* 1971 p. 600, 1972 p. 627, and 1973 p. 596; for a more accurate comparison, these figures should be discounted by the rate of inflation for each country. Rates of inflation in consumer prices are not available before 1964, and amounted to 24% in both countries over the period 1965–70 (*United Nations Yearbook of Labour Statistics* 1973 pp. 700–1).
14. *ibid.*
15. *ibid.*
16. *United Nations Yearbook of National Accounts Statistics* 1972, vol. 2 pp. 12, 339; per capita figures obtained by dividing the total by the estimated population for 1970 given in *United Nations Demographic Yearbook* 1970.
17. Sierra Leone, *Annual Statistical Digest 1971*, Table 50; *West Africa*, 22 April 1974, p. 474.
18. *A & A Directory and Who's Who in Liberia, 1971* (Monrovia 1971) p. 107.
19. J. G. Liebenow, *Liberia, The Evolution of Privilege* (Cornell 1969) pp. 113–15.
20. *Liberian Age*, 7 February 1963; *West Africa*, 9 April 1973 p. 482; 11 June 1973 p. 790; 18 June 1973 p. 828; 2 July 1973 p. 867.
21. Liebenow, *op. cit.*, pp. 215–16.
22. The two principal studies of Sierra Leone politics during the decolonisation and early independence periods are J. R. Cartwright, *Politics in Sierra Leone 1947–1967* (Toronto 1970), and M. Kilson, *Political Change in a West African State, A Study of the Modernization Process in Sierra Leone* (Harvard 1966); developments since independence are covered in C. Allen, 'Sierra Leone Politics since Independence', *African Affairs*, vol. 67, October

1968, pp. 305–29, C. Clapham, 'Sierra Leone: Civilian Rule and the New Republic', *The World Today*, February 1972, pp. 82–91, and H. J. Fisher, 'Elections and Coups in Sierra Leone', *Journal of Modern African Studies*, vol. 7 no. 4, 1969, pp. 611–36.

Chapter 3. Resources

1. Definitions of 'the plural society' vary considerably in strictness. At one extreme, any society incorporating distinct cultural sections may be called plural, and in this sense of the term Sierra Leone would qualify. At the other extreme, pluralism requires the hegemony of a distinct and exclusive cultural minority imposing its rule by force on other sections, and in this sense even Liberia would scarcely qualify, for though there is a dominant minority, it allows participation by other groups within the common institutions of the state. Many accounts refer to Liberia as a plural society, though in doing so they are apt to exaggerate the exclusiveness of Americo-Liberian hegemony. For a discussion of the subject, incorporating definitions of varying strictness and passing references to Liberia, see L. Kuper & M. G. Smith, eds., *Pluralism in Africa* (University of California 1969), especially chs. 1 and 2. For a more thoroughgoing analysis of Liberia as a plural society, see M. F. Lofchie 'The Americo-Liberian Oligarchy: A Conflict Model', *Africa Today*, vol. 17 no. 2, March–April 1970, pp. 11–16; this discussion is, I feel, rather overinfluenced by the author's experience of Zanzibar.
2. See Amos C. Sawyer, *Social Stratification and Orientations to National Development in Liberia* (Ph.D. Thesis, Northwestern University 1973). Sawyer notes a general lack of national development orientations at all levels of the stratification system.
3. Liebenow, *op. cit.*, p. 158.
4. The phrases 'Negroes or persons of Negro descent' are specified in the *Constitution of the Republic of Liberia*, 1847, Article 5 Section 13, and 'person of negro african descent' in *The Constitution of Sierra Leone*, 1971, Article 21.
5. For the Creole/Protectorate division and the 1951 election see Cartwright, *op. cit.*, pp. 52–4; for the role of Freemasonry in Creole politics, see A. Cohen, 'The Politics of Ritual Secrecy', *Man*, vol. 6, 1971, pp. 427–48.
6. See J. S. Sinclair, 'Perceptions of Social Stratification among Sub-elite of Sierra Leone', a paper delivered at the Toronto Conference on Sierra Leone Studies, Toronto 1971.
7. Dr Karefa-Smart, a Koko by parentage brought up in Temneland, provides an interesting example of the 'declared' ethnic identity discussed in the last paragraph (A. Lewally-Taylor, pers. comm.).
8. Liebenow, *op. cit.*, pp. 135–41.
9. See Cartwright, *op. cit.*, pp. 98–100.
10. M. Fraenkel, for example, uses the term 'class' widely in her excellent study of social relationships in Monrovia, *Tribe and Class in Monrovia* (Oxford 1964).
11. See N. O. Leighton, *The Lebanese Middleman in Sierra Leone – The Case of a Non-Indigenous Trading Minority and their Role in Political Development* (Ph.D. Dissertation, Indiana University 1971) pp. 255–8.
12. There is little available material on trade unions in either Liberia or Sierra

Leone; for Liberia, see Liebenow, *op. cit.*, pp. 87–90, and Clower, *op. cit.*, pp. 280–4.

13. For Kono politics, see V. Minikin, *Local Politics in Kono District Sierra Leone, 1945–1970* (Ph.D. Thesis, University of Birmingham 1971) and F. M. Hayward, 'The Development of a Radical Political Organisation in the Bush: A Case Study in Sierra Leone', *Canadian Journal of African Studies*, vol. 6 no. 1, 1972, pp. 1–28.
14. For a perceptive discussion of 'kwiness' in rural Liberia, see J. Gay, 'Continuities of Culture in Liberian Society', *Liberian Research Association Journal*, vol. 3 no. 2, 1971.
15. See Kilson, *op. cit.*, pp. 232–3, and Cartwright, *op. cit.*, pp. 97–164.
16. See Liebenow, *op. cit.*, pp. 102–7, and Kilson, *op. cit.*, pp. 76–7.
17. One public indication of hostility has been student cheering of the defence and booing of the prosecution at treason trials, both in 1968 (Liebenow, *op. cit.*, p. 216) and in 1973 (*West Africa*, 2 July 1973, p. 867). Student publications which emerged after the liberalisation of the press by the Tolbert government were also overwhelmingly critical.
18. See Kilson, *op. cit.*, pp. 237–8, and J. R. Cartwright, 'Party Competition in a Developing Nation: The Basis of Support for an Opposition in Sierra Leone', *J. Commonwealth Political Studies*, vol. 10 no. 1, 1972, pp. 71–90.
19. See Minikin, *op. cit.*, chs. 4–6.
20. The only authentic expression of Liberian populism of which I have been able to find evidence is the Aborigines' Liberation Front, which issued pamphlets attacking both the Americo-Liberians and assimilated hinterlanders in 1968 and 1969.
21. See ch. 2, note 16.
22. *United Nations Yearbook of Labour Statistics*, 1973, pp. 47 and 53.
23. The importance of patronage in helping a Prime Minister to maintain a parliamentary majority is particularly clear in Albert Margai's success in forestalling opposition to his appointment as Prime Minister in 1964; see Cartwright, *op. cit.*, pp. 185–7.

Chapter 4. Rules

1. The concept of rules used here is adapted from that outlined by F. G. Bailey, *op. cit.*, ch. 2; for a rather different concept of rules, see P. Winch, *The Idea of a Social Science* (Routledge and Kegan Paul 1958).
2. The Constitution of the Republic of Liberia, 1847 (with amendments), and the Constitution of Sierra Leone, 1961 are conveniently accessible in A. J. Peaslee, *Constitutions of Nations, vol. I – Africa* (Nijhoff 1965) pp. 422–32 and 715–71; The Constitution of Sierra Leone, 1971, is published as a Supplement to *The Sierra Leone Gazette*, vol. CII, Freetown 1971.
3. This is the provision under which Tubman renewed his Presidency for successive four-year terms from 1952 until 1971; the restriction of tenure to a single eight-year term has been proposed by President Tolbert.
4. Until 1972, Liberian Ministries were known as Departments, and their heads as Secretaries, following United States nomenclature; Sierra Leone Ministries were called Departments under the NRC, when members of the Council exercised ministerial responsibilities.
5. See A. Cohen, 'The Creole Way of Death', a paper delivered at the Toronto

Conference on Sierra Leone Studies, Toronto 1971; and 'The Politics of Ritual Secrecy', *loc. cit.*

6. The Poro Society (for men) and Sande Society (for women) are important social institutions in much of Sierra Leone and central and northern Liberia; their primary function is educational – to transmit values and customs to succeeding generations – but they also act as agencies of communal solidarity, and hence for political identity and conflict-resolution; for further discussion of their political role, see K. Little, 'The Political Function of the Poro', *Africa*, vol. 35 no. 4, 1965, pp. 349–65, and vol. 36 no. 1, 1966, pp. 62–72.
7. See Cartwright, 'Party Competition in a Developing Nation', *loc. cit.*
8. J. G. Liebenow, 'Liberia', in G. M. Carter, ed., *African One-Party States* (Cornell 1962), and *op. cit.*, pp. 137–41.
9. Cartwright, *op. cit.*, pp. 97, 164; the figures are not quite comparable, since those for 1957 refer to all MPs representing provincial constituencies, while those for 1962 refer to MPs of provincial origin in any constituency.
10. *ibid.*, pp. 164–6.
11. The effect of the prize structure at the local level on patterns of central–local linkage has been superbly argued by W. L. Barrows in his study of Kenema District, *Local-Level Politics in Sierra Leone: Alliances in Kenema District* (Ph.D. Thesis, Yale University 1971) ch. 1; the situation in Kono is examined in Minikin, *op. cit.*, and APC support in the north in Cartwright, 'Party Competition in a Developing Nation', *loc. cit.*

Chapter 5. Political Allocation at the Centre

1. See the chart of family connections in Liebenow, *op. cit.*, p. 139.
2. See Tables 1–3, pp. 48–51.
3. A vignette from *The Liberian Star*, 17 October 1973, helps to set the scene: 'The Past Grand Master of Masons, McKinley A. De Shield (Postmaster General and National Chairman of the True Whig Party) yesterday at the Executive Mansion presented a Sash of the Masonic Craft to President Tolbert as a belated birthday gift. Mr Tolbert whose 60th birthday, was 13th May of this year, is Past Grand Master of Masons. Present during the ceremony were Past Grand Master Richard A. Henries (Speaker of the House of Representatives); Grand Master E. Jonathan Goodridge (Minister of Local Government) and Deputy Grand Master James E. Greene (Vice-President).' These four officials are all leading members of the Americo-Liberian community, and this ceremony may be seen not only as a mark of respect to the President but more as a public display of their shared position with him in a communal organisation.
4. Liebenow, *op. cit.*, pp. 62–3.
5. W. H. Riker, in *The Theory of Political Coalitions* (Yale 1962), chs. 2–3, examines in formal theoretical terms the reasons why coalitions tend to break up when they become larger than is needed for them to retain control of government; his discussion is very relevant to Sierra Leone during the period of open competition between parties.
6. Cartwright, *op. cit.*, pp. 108–17.
7. See Clapham, 'Sierra Leone: Civilian Rule and the New Republic', *loc. cit.*
8. Though an alliance between the UDP and the SLPP was for tactical reasons denied on both sides, prominent members of both parties have confirmed

to me that they had such an arrangement in mind; several UDP supporters stood as SLPP candidates in the 1973 election.

9. See Allen, 'Sierra Leone Politics since Independence', *loc. cit.*
10. *The People*, Freetown, 24 June 1972.
11. Liebenow, *op. cit.*, pp. 99–100, 135–41; see also S. S. Hlophe, 'The Role of the Urban Family in the Emergence of the Modern Political Class Structure in Liberia', paper presented at the 6th annual Liberian Studies Conference, Madison, April 1974.
12. Cartwright, *op. cit.*, pp. 172–3.
13. *Daily Mail*, Freetown, May 1968, passim.
14. Republic of Liberia, *Presidential Papers 1971–1972* (Monrovia n.d.) pp. 5–40.
15. Cartwright, *op. cit.*, p. 179.
16. 'Coercion', as I use the term here, means force used by the government to maintain itself in power; 'violence' means force used against or independently of the government, including its use by official organisations against the government in the case, say, of a military coup.
17. Liberian Information Service, *The Plot that Failed* (London 1959), and Liebenow, *op. cit.*, pp. 113–18.
18. *The Liberian Age*, Monrovia, 7 February 1970.
19. *West Africa*, 24 October 1970, p. 1264.
20. *The Liberian Age*, 22 February 1963 and 11 March 1963.
21. See ch. 2, note 20.
22. *West Africa*, 2 September 1974, p. 1087.
23. Cartwright, *op. cit.*, p. 136.
24. *ibid.*, pp. 230–4, 244.
25. *ibid.*, p. 243.
26. *West Africa*, 19 August 1974, p. 1030; 26 August 1974, p. 1057.
27. Notably Mr Julius Cole.
28. For the background to this affair, see Clapham, 'Sierra Leone: Civilian Rule and the New Republic', *loc. cit.*
29. *West Africa*, 25 November 1974, p. 1443; 28 July 1975, p. 878; 11 August 1975, p. 947.
30. From copies shown to the author; the Aborigines' Liberation Front has brought itself to public notice only through these pamphlets, which appear to be the work of primary school leavers rather than of a radical intelligentsia.
31. *West Africa*, 15 March 1969, p. 311, quoting a report to Amnesty International.
32. For example, the East African mutinies of 1964, or the French intervention in Gabon in the same year.
33. The only published reports which I can find are in the opposition newspaper *The People*, for 17 June 1972, 1, 8, 15 and 22 July 1972, 16 December 1972, and 27 January 1973.
34. See Cartwright, *op. cit.*, p. 282.
35. *ibid.*, pp. 216–18.
36. Cohen, 'The Politics of Ritual Secrecy', *loc. cit.*

Chapter 6. Centre and Periphery

1. Barrows, *op. cit.*, ch. 2.

2. Fulton, *op. cit.*, ch. 6.
3. Chiefdom Councillors were formerly known as Tribal Authorities, and the abbreviation TA is still in use.
4. From a handout issued by the Electoral Commission, Monrovia, at the Bong/Kpai chieftaincy election in October 1973.
5. I have adopted the convention of combining in this way the name of the County (in Liberia) or District (in Sierra Leone) with that of the Chiefdom.
6. Minikin, *op. cit.*, passim; Barrows, *op. cit.*, ch. 5.
7. Port Loko/Koya is the obvious case; see R. Tangri, 'Aspects of Violence in Contemporary Sierra Leone Chiefdoms', *Local Government and Politics in Sierra Leone*, forthcoming.
8. Barrows, *op. cit.*, ch. 5.
9. See note 7, above, and *Daily Mail*, Freetown, 18 September 1973.
10. For the underlying principles of coalition formation, see Riker, *op. cit.*
11. For example, see the Kenema/Kandu-Leppiama election of November 1969, described in Barrows, *op. cit.*, ch. 5.
12. The result is reported in *Liberian Star*, Monrovia, 11 October 1973; other information on both these elections comes from interviews conducted on the spot in October and November 1973.
13. Clower, *op. cit.*, pp. 19–20, 333–4.
14. For the colonial period, see Sir Herbert Cox, *Report of Commission of Enquiry into the Disturbances in the Provinces, November 1955–March 1956* (Freetown, 1956); for more recent cases, see the Auditor-General's report summarised in *West Africa*, 30 November 1968, p. 1422, and 28 March 1970, p. 343. Exactions by chiefs are a constant theme in Kilson, *op. cit.*, especially chs. 2, 4, 12 and 13.
15. *West Africa*, 10 March 1975, p. 293 and 17 March 1975, p. 321; see also C. Viswasam, *Sierra Leone Local Government in the Chiefdoms* (Freetown 1973) and R. Tangri, *op. cit.*
16. See Minikin, *op. cit.*, especially ch. 4.
17. Sierra Leone, The Tonkolili and Marampa Supplementary Agreement (1973) (Ratification) Act, 1973, Schedule 1, Art. 2., *The Sierra Leone Gazette*, Supplement to vol. CIV no. 52, 1973.
18. Barrows, *op. cit.*, ch. 5.
19. From a list supplied by the Ministry of Interior, Freetown.
20. *Provinces Handbook 1969/70* (Freetown 1970).
21. See Kenema/Dama and Kenema/Kandu-Leppiama, in Barrows, *op. cit.*, ch. 5.
22. Cartwright, *op. cit.*, pp. 196–7.
23. See Barrows, *op. cit.*, ch. 3.
24. *ibid.* ch. 7; see also 'Aspects of Violence in Contemporary Sierra Leone Chiefdoms', in Tangri, *op. cit.*
25. *The People*, Freetown, 7 June 1972.
26. Sierra Leone, *Report of the Beoku Betts Commission of Inquiry on the Special Coffee Deal of the Sierra Leone Produce Marketing Board 1967* (Freetown 1967), and *Report of the Forster Commission of Inquiry on Assets of Ex-Ministers and Ex-Deputy Ministers* (Freetown 1968).
27. Barrows, *op. cit.*, ch. 3.
28. Symptomatic of this is the fact that the two outstanding studies of local politics in Sierra Leone, by Barrows and Minikin, make no reference to the

Regional Minister, Provincial Secretary, or District Officer at all. See Barrows and Minikin, *op. cit.*

29. Cartwright, *op. cit.*, pp. 218–19.
30. *West Africa*, 10 March 1975, p. 293.
31. *ibid.*, 17 March 1975, p. 321.
32. This figure has been calculated from the *Administrative Postings* lists issued monthly for the Sierra Leone civil service.
33. Montserrado County had no Superintendent from about 1913 until 1973, but came directly under the central government.
34. *Liberian Star*, 6 November 1973.
35. *ibid.*, 19 October 1973.
36. *ibid.*, 3 and 4 October 1973, 6 November 1973; *Liberian Age*, 19 October 1973.
37. See p. 12.
38. Republic of Liberia, Ministry of Internal Affairs, *Report for 1970–71*, p. 32; this refers to the dismissal of Supt. Ballayan of Lofa County.
39. For biographies of Jones and Greaves, see Research Institute of the Friedrich-Ebert-Stiftung *African Biographies* (Bonn-Bad Godesberg 1967 et seq.).
40. These percentages have been arrived at by compiling a list of the names and origins of officials in each County in October and November 1973, including County Commissioners, the local representatives of central government ministries; local court judges, and army commanders, but excluding Senators, Representatives, and Paramount Chiefs; they comprise 32 officials for Bong County, 23 for Cape Mount, and 43 for Lofa.
41. See Barrows, *op. cit.*, ch. 4, and Minikin, *op. cit.*, chs. 5 and 6.
42. Minikin, *op. cit.*, ch. 5.
43. Cartwright, *op. cit.*, pp. 218–19.
44. Barrows, *op. cit.*, ch. 4.
45. Tangri, *op. cit.*, ch. 4.
46. Cartwright, *op. cit.*, pp. 156–7.
47. For the means which enabled the APC to maintain itself in opposition, see Cartwright, 'Party Competition in a Developing Nation', *loc. cit.*
48. For the selection of APC candidates in 1967, see Cartwright, *op. cit.*, p. 246.
49. For the application of 'machine politics' to African political parties, see H. Bienen, 'Political Parties and Political Machines in Africa', in M. F. Lofchie, ed., *The State of the Nations* (California 1971); the TWP is more readily analysable as a machine than most African political parties, since the ideological element in it is particularly low, and the transactions which it carries out have had time to become regularised and accepted.
50. M. Lowenkopf, *Political Modernization and Integration in Liberia* (Ph.D. Thesis, London University 1969) pp. 138–40.
51. Cartwright, *op. cit.*, pp. 160–1.
52. For examples, see Minikin, *op. cit.*, ch. 6 and Barrows, *op. cit.*, ch. 5.
53. The ministers were A. B. S. Janneh (Social Welfare), S. A. T. Koroma (Agriculture), B. Mansaray (Interior), and F. B. Turay (Lands), of whom the first three were well-established local politicians from the Northern Province.
54. Reports of County Commissioners, quoted from A. H. Williams, *Annual Report, Department of Internal Affairs, R.L.* (Monrovia 1968) pp. 56, 57, 60.

55. See Barrows, *op. cit.*, ch. 4; this trend is the local echo of a tendency for government revenues to be sucked up increasingly in administrative costs, which is apparent throughout Africa; see I. Wallerstein, 'The Range of Choice: Constraints on the Policies of Governments of Contemporary African Independent States', in Lofchie, *op. cit.*

Chapter 7. Aspects of Political Economy

1. For an excellent discussion of economic constraints on African governments, see Wallerstein, 'The Range of Choice', *loc. cit.*
2. For demonstrations against Foulahs, see *West Africa*, 15 November 1969, p. 1387; for strikes, see Liebenow, *op. cit.*, pp. 89–90; *The Liberian Age*, Monrovia, 5 July 1963; *Daily Mail*, Freetown, 6 November 1969.
3. Information for Liberia from Clower, *op. cit.*, Table 23, and *Quarterly Statistical Bulletin, Summary for 1972, op. cit.*, Table 2.3 (1972 figures are estimates); for Sierra Leone *Estimates of Revenues and Expenditure 1969–70* (Freetown 1969), and *Estimates of Revenue and Expenditure 1973–74* (Freetown 1973).
4. Clower, *op. cit.*, ch. 6.
5. R. G. Saylor, *The Economic System of Sierra Leone* (Duke 1967) p. 204.
6. Cartwright, *op. cit.*, pp. 150, 247.
7. For contractor finance projects under Albert Margai, see *West Africa*, 12 April 1969, p. 422; this account, given by his political opponents, may be exaggerated. The inefficiency of state corporations and of joint ventures with government participation was criticised by the APC Minister of Finance in 1975 (see *West Africa*, 7 July 1975, p. 791).
8. See Saylor, *op. cit.*, p. 205, for Sierra Leone.
9. See, for example, *West Africa*, 21 April 1975, p. 461.
10. Cartwright, *op. cit.*, pp. 279–80.
11. Kilson, *op. cit.*, pp. 207–9.
12. See *Report of the Forster Commission, op. cit.*
13. A Bebler, *Military Rule in Africa: Dahomey, Ghana, Sierra Leone, and Mali* (Praeger 1973) p. 187.
14. N. A. Cox-George, *Report on African Participation in the Commerce of Sierra Leone* (Freetown 1958).
15. Saylor, *op. cit.*, p. 96.
16. *West Africa*, 9 August 1969, p. 939.
17. *West Africa*, 15 November 1969, p. 1387.
18. *West Africa*, 7 March 1970, p. 271.
19. As so often, the only newspaper to raise the issue was *The People*, 24 June 1972, 20 January 1973.
20. For the late Stephen Tolbert's Mesurado Group, see 'The Brothers Tolbert', in *The Financial Times*, London, 24 November 1974.
21. Lowenkopf, *op. cit.*, p. 321, and *Liberia Official Gazette*, vol. 91, November–December 1967.
22. N. O. Leighton, *The Lebanese Middleman in Sierra Leone: the Case of a Non-Indigenous Trading Minority and their Role in Political Development* (Ph.D. Dissertation, Indiana University 1971) pp. 280–6; Leighton quotes a payment of Le50,000 exacted from Lebanese in Kono for the benefit of Albert Margai in 1966.
23. *Constitution of the Republic of Liberia, loc. cit.*, Article 7 section 13.

24. Leighton, *op. cit.*, pp. 254–9.
25. *The Sierra Leone Nationality and Citizenship Act, 1962.*
26. *The Sierra Leone Citizenship Act, 1973.*
27. *West Africa*, 18 December 1972, p. 1707.
28. See Leighton, *op. cit.*, conclusion.
29. Co-operatives are far better established in Lofa County, especially in Kissi and Gbandi Chiefdoms, than in other areas.
30. See the Statistical Appendix.
31. *Daily Mail*, Freetown, 10 May 1968.
32. *The Tonkolili and Marampa Supplementary Agreement (1956) Ratification Act, 1956*; and *Tonkolili and Marampa Supplementary Agreement (1973) (Ratification) Act*, 1973.
33. Figures supplied by the Resident Director, Delco, Freetown November 1973.
34. Information in this paragraph supplied by the Ministry of Planning and Economic Affairs, Monrovia.
35. Information supplied by the Ministry of Finance, Monrovia.
36. Department of Planning and Economic Affairs, R.L., *Economic Survey 1967* (Monrovia 1968) p. 50; of the total value added in the iron ore industry of $82.9m in 1966, $22.9 accrued to Liberian factors of production ($8.9m to Liberian labour, $4.2m to Liberian capital, and $9.2m to government revenue); in the rubber industry, 66% of value added accrued to Liberian factors ($17.7m out of $26.6m), so that with a much smaller value added, it made a comparable contribution to the Liberian economy.
37. Saylor, *op. cit.*, p. 140; Clower, *op. cit.*, p. 203.
38. See *African Development*, 'Liberia 125 Years of Independence' Supplement, 1972, p. 29.
39. *West Africa*, 17 February 1975, p. 203.
40. Cartwright, *op. cit.*, p. 150.
41. *African Development, op. cit.*, p. 29 contrasts the officially declared figure of $5.7m for Liberian diamond exports in 1971 with an actual figure of $28.7m.
42. Information supplied by the Bureau of Lands and Surveys, Monrovia, in October 1973, and confirmed by informants in Grand Cape Mount County.
43. Information gained during a visit to Kpai Chiefdom, November 1973.
44. Lowenkopf, *op. cit.*, pp. 71–3.
45. Liebenow, *op. cit.*, pp. 66–8.
46. Clower, *op. cit.*, pp. 296–8.
47. Saylor, *op. cit.*, pp. 50–4.
48. See M. H. Husain, *Report to the Government of Sierra Leone on Customary Land Tenure in the Context of a Developing Agricultural Economy* (Rome: F.A.O. Report no. 1853, 1964); changes in provincial land tenure arrangements have frequently been proposed, but no government has yet been prepared to alienate the chiefdom authorities by implementing them.
49. Clower, *op. cit.*, p. 164; *The Liberian Age*, 5 July 1963; personal enquiry, 1969. There are no figures for retail prices before 1964; Clower, *op. cit.*, estimates an increase of 37% between 1950 and 1960; *United Nations Yearbook of Labour Statistics 1973*, p. 701, gives an increase of 25% between 1964 and 1969.

50. W. R. Tolbert, *Toward a Brave, New Liberia: Independence Day Message July 26, 1973* (Monrovia 1973).
51. Saylor, *op. cit.*
52. Cartwright, *op. cit.*, pp. 206, 214; *Report of the Beoku Betts Commission*, *op. cit.*
53. Fisher, 'Elections and Coups in Sierra Leone 1967', *loc. cit.*, p. 618.
54. See Figures 2–4.
55. From official circulars to buying agents from the LPMC and SLPMB, October–November 1973; the Liberian figures were also advertised in the newspapers. The exchange rate is here reckoned at Le1.00 = $1.20, though precise rates fluctuate with the £ sterling, to which the Leone is pegged.
56. *West Africa*, 7 January 1974, p. 22; 30 September 1974, p. 1202; 18 November 1974, p. 1416.
57. From interviews conducted in Lofa County, October–November 1973; I could not discover the official Guinean buying price in Silys, but the comparison between the two countries evidently assumes an exchange at the open market rate, rather than the official rate for the heavily controlled Guinean currency.
58. See, for example, *West Africa*, 19 May 1975, p. 586.
59. Saylor, *op. cit.*, pp. 100–26; Saylor, who is anxious to prove the deleterious effects of SLPMB intervention, may exaggerate its role, against other possible factors such as land-holding and the attractions of emigration to the Kono diamond fields; however, his general conclusions are strongly supported in an article by J. Levi in *Ford Research Institute Studies* (Stanford 1975) reviewed in *West Africa*, 19 May 1975, p. 581.
60. I. T. D. Amarchree, *Agricultural Innovation in Rural Liberia: A Study of Farmers among the Kissi*, roneo, Monrovia 1970.
61. Saylor, *op. cit.*, pp. 106–7; *West Africa*, 25 November 1974, p. 1443.

Chapter 8. Concluding Review

1. Huntington, *op. cit.*, chs. 1 and 7. There is no question about the absence of a 'green uprising' in Liberia, where government is still dominated by urban elites, but Sierra Leone is more of a problem. The defeat of the NCSL by the SLPP in 1951 falls neatly into Huntington's pattern of mobilisation by party competition, and the defeat of the SLPP by the APC in 1967 may be regarded as furthering this pattern by extending participation beyond the rural elites which dominated the SLPP. This does not however lead to the integration of mass participation and urban leadership, but rather to an alliance between them which may be broken when (with the decay of electoral institutions) leaders no longer need rural support, and when that support is withdrawn. In this, the praetorian situation, the work of mobilising the rural masses into political institutions remains to be done again. This can only be fully achieved, and the 'green uprising' consummated, when rural and urban structures become so closely enmeshed that the gap between them ceases to exist.
2. Huntington, *op. cit.*, ch. 1; and 'Political Development and Political Decay', *World Politics*, vol. XVII no. 3, 1965.
3. MacIntyre, 'Is a Science of Comparative Politics Possible?', *loc. cit.*
4. See S. E. Finer, 'Almond's Concept of "The Political System": A Textual Critique', *Government and Opposition*, vol. 5 no. 1, 1970, pp. 3–21.

INDEX

References to Liberia and to Sierra Leone are marked (L) and (SL) respectively.